Agile Approaches on Large Projects in Large Organizations

Brian Hobbs and Yvan Petit
School of Management, University of Quebec at Montreal

Library of Congress Cataloging-in-Publication Data has been applied for.

ISBN: 978-1-62825-175-3

Published by: Project Management Institute, Inc.
　　　　　　　14 Campus Boulevard
　　　　　　　Newtown Square, Pennsylvania 19073-3299 USA
　　　　　　　Phone: +610-356-4600
　　　　　　　Fax: +610-482-9971
　　　　　　　Email: customercare@pmi.org
　　　　　　　Internet: www.PMI.org

To inquire about discounts for resale or educational purposes, please contact the PMI Book Service Center.

　　　　　　　PMI Book Service Center
　　　　　　　P.O. Box 932683, Atlanta, GA 31193-2683 USA
　　　　　　　Phone: 1+866-276-4764 (within the U.S. or Canada) or
　　　　　　　+1-770-280-4129 (globally)
　　　　　　　Fax: +1-770-280-4113
　　　　　　　Email: info@bookorders.pmi.org

10 9 8 7 6 5 4 3 2

Table of Contents

List of Tables

List of Acronyms

ABB	Asea Brown Boveri
ASM	Agile Scaling Model
CIO	Chief Information Officer
CMMI	Capability Maturity Model Integration
DAD	Disciplined Agile Delivery
IT	Information Technology
IEEE	Institute of Electrical and Electronics Engineers
LeSS	Large-Scale Scrum
PMI	Project Management Institute
(PMI-ACP)®	PMI Agile Certified Practitioner
PMO	Project Management Office
PO	Product Owner
QA	Quality Assurance
SAFe	Scaled Agile Framework
XP	Extreme Programming

Executive Summary

Agile methods have taken software development by storm, but have been primarily applied to projects in what is referred to as the "agile sweet spot," which consists of small colocated teams working on small, noncritical, green field, in-house software projects with stable architectures and simple governance rules. The use of agile on large projects in large organizations is a relatively new phenomenon for which clear guidance is not available. There are conflicts between agile principles and traditional software development in large bureaucratic organizations. Organizations are experimenting, as shown by the extreme variability of the responses to most of the survey questions introduced in this study. On average, large organizations have been using agile on large projects for three years. With an average project duration of one-and-a-half years, a large number of organizations have completed only a small number of large agile projects. Many large organizations are therefore still at a stage of experimental implementation.

Because many large organizations are currently experimenting with agile, the results are somewhat paradoxical in that some features are common to almost all observations, while others show extreme variability. The common features include use of Scrum methodology and agile coaches as well as the disregard of the agile principle of emergent architecture.

One of the most important emergent phenomena from a project management perspective is the modifications being made to the role of the project manager. One element that is relatively clear is that self-organizing Scrum development teams have a major role in the detailed planning and monitoring of project execution and that project managers are, therefore, devoting less effort to this type of activity. Project managers typically have a role in the coordination of multiple development teams. However, some contexts report that project managers are putting more effort into this activity, while others report that they are putting less. It is not clear under what conditions each of these tendencies is prevalent. In many organizations, the project manager role has become more strategic and more centered on stakeholder management. In a minority of cases, the project manager role has been abolished. As this is an emergent phenomenon, it is too early to know what the long-term effects on the project manager role will be. As the situation is evolving quickly, more research will be required.

CHAPTER 1

Introduction

Agile has taken software development by storm since the publication of the *Agile Manifesto* (Agile Alliance, 2001). In recent years, agile methodologies have become highly prevalent in the software industry (Abrahamsson, Conboy, & Xiaofeng, 2009; Dingsøyr, Nerur, Balijepally, & Moe, 2012). Today, it is one of the hottest topics in project management; Project Management Institute (PMI) has created the PMI Agile Certified Practitioner (PMI-ACP)® certification and *Project Management Journal*® has published a special issue on the topic. (Note that the special issue and this research monograph will likely be published at approximately the same time. For a summary of the present research, see Hobbs and Petit [2017].)

Although there have been multiple attempts to apply agile principles to non-software projects (Conforto, Salum, Amaral, da Silva, & de Almeida, 2014; Highsmith, 2003; Petit & Levesque, 2015), this research is limited to the field of software development—the field where agile has become prominent. It focuses on two levels of analysis: the individual project and the organizational context in which projects are carried out. The agile literature has focused almost exclusively on the former, while almost completely ignoring the latter.

The advantages of using agile identified in the literature include: a working environment that supports creativity and productivity, rapid adaptation to change, and value for the customer because of better identification of needs and priorities and faster multiple deliveries of functionalities (Schwaber, 2004; Thomke & Reinertsen, 1998). These advantages are more readily obtained with certain types of projects in certain contexts. Kruchten (2013) identified what is referred to as the "agile sweet spot," which consists of small colocated teams working on small, noncritical, green field, in-house software projects with stable architectures and simple governance rules. Most of the writings on agile report on situations that are close to the sweet spot. Projects and contexts with the opposite characteristics are examined much less extensively in the literature. Studies of projects outside the sweet spot have revealed that they are much more problematic. Leffingwell (2010) showed that there are a number of impediments to the scaling of these practices in large multisite, multi-customer, multi-project organizations. For more than five years, larger organizations have been adopting agile approaches and struggling to scale from a few agile teams to an organization-wide implementation of agile. In a survey of 3,880 participants, VersionOne (2016) found that organizations are continuing to scale agile beyond single teams and single projects and that more energy is put into scaling agile across the enterprise. However, little has been reported in the literature on either the practices employed on individual projects or the interplay between agile practices and the accompanying organizational arrangements (Kettunen, 2007) despite the fact that this is considered one of the top research topics among practitioners (Dingsøyr & Moe, 2013, 2014; Freudenberg & Sharp, 2010). The overall objective of the present research is to fill this gap by examining projects and contexts that are not in the agile sweet spot, specifically large software projects in large organizations.

The research question at the project level is: *What challenges are encountered when applying agile methods to large multiteam software projects and what practices have been developed to alleviate these challenges*? The literature that has examined these questions has most often taken an approach that contrasts and/or mixes agile and traditional project management approaches (Boehm & Turner, 2003, 2004, 2005; Conforto, Salum, Amaral, da Silva, & de Almeida, 2014; Conforto, Rebentisch, & Amaral, 2014; Sommer, Hedegaard, Dukovska-Popovska, & Steger-Jensen, 2015; Špundak, 2014). The present research aims to go beyond this somewhat simplistic approach based on a rich description of practice in specific contexts.

At the organizational level, the research examines the implementation of agile approaches in large organizations as it has unfolded over time by examining implementation strategies. The adoption of agile by a large, complex organization requires experimentation and adaptation of the agile practices to the organization's structure, culture, product/service strategy, human resource management policies, customer interfaces, project roles, and governance structures, including program and project portfolio management. At the same time, the organizational context is influenced by the implementation of agile. The research question at the organizational level is: *How does the context of large, complex organizations affect the adaptation and adoption of agile approaches and vice versa?*

CHAPTER 2

Literature Review

2.1 Agile Approaches

Agile methodologies are specific approaches to implement flexibility in the project management process, which have been designed in response to the specific challenges of the software industry (i.e., high uncertainty, ill-defined requirements, short development cycle, and no physical deliverable) (Agile Alliance, 2001; Lindvall et al., 2004). For example, Gruver, Young, and Fulghum (2013) describe how Hewlett-Packard went from spending 20% of their project budget on plans to 5%, the argument being that plans needed for business decisions do not require the detail and precision of traditional project plans and that the resources are put to better use developing the product rather than producing detailed plans that will be wrong. Conboy (2009) conceptualizes the agile approach from two related concepts: flexibility and leanness. Agile methodology was inspired by the flexible mass production systems, led by the Toyota production system of the 1950s. It further evolved into the lean manufacturing concept, which then became *lean thinking* within the quality movement (Abrahamsson, Warsta, Siponen, & Ronkainen, 2003;

Carstens, Richardson, & Smith, 2013). The quality movement paved the way for agile software development. All of the agile approaches share common values and principles stated in the *Agile Manifesto* (Agile Alliance, 2001) and subsequent publications by authors of the manifesto (Levin, 2012; Schwaber, 2007). Of these methods, Scrum and Extreme Programming (XP) are by far the best known and most widely used (VersionOne, 2016).

The authors of the *Agile Manifesto* did not try to define what they meant by agile. Instead they proposed 12 principles and four values (see Table 1) that identify some areas where the focus of software projects should be changed.

Laanti, Similä, Abrahamsson, and Delta (2013) analyze how subsequent definitions of agile put more or less emphasis on some of the items identified in the manifesto. Kettunen (2009b) and Laanti et al. (2013) identify 10 definitions of agile ranging from

Table 1: Summary of the *Agile Manifesto*

Four values of the *Agile Manifesto*
1. Individuals and interactions over processes and tools.
2. Working software over comprehensive documentation.
3. Customer collaboration over contract negotiation.
4. Responding to change over following a plan.
That is, while there is value in the items on the right, we value the items on the left more.

Twelve principles behind the *Agile Manifesto*
1. Our highest priority is to satisfy the customer through early and continuous delivery of valuable software.
2. Welcome changing requirements, even late in development. Agile processes harness change for the customer's competitive advantage.
3. Deliver working software frequently, from a couple of weeks to a couple of months, with a preference to the shorter timescale.
4. Business people and developers must work together daily throughout the project.
5. Build projects around motivated individuals. Give them the environment and support they need, and trust them to get the job done.
6. The most efficient and effective method of conveying information to and within a development team is face-to-face conversation.
7. Working software is the primary measure of progress.
8. Agile processes promote sustainable development. The sponsors, developers, and users should be able to maintain a constant pace indefinitely.
9. Continuous attention to technical excellence and good design enhances agility.
10. Simplicity—the art of maximizing the amount of work not done is essential.
11. The best architectures, requirements, and designs emerge from self-organizing teams.
12. At regular intervals, the team reflects on how to become more effective, then tunes and adjusts its behavior accordingly.

"rapid and flexible response to change" (Larman, 2004), which primarily focuses on the adaptation to change in agile, to the Institute of Electrical and Electronics Engineers (IEEE) putting more emphasis on the iterative nature of agile as the *"capability to accommodate uncertain or changing needs up to a late stage of the development (until the start of the last iterative development cycle of the release)"* (Laanti et al., 2013). However, we prefer the more comprehensive definition of Ambler (2009), which covers the main principles included in the manifesto:

> *Agile software development is an evolutionary (iterative and incremental) approach which regularly produces high quality software in a cost effective and timely manner via a value driven lifecycle. It is performed in a highly collaborative, disciplined, and self-organizing manner with active stakeholder participation to ensure that the team understands and addresses the changing needs of its stakeholders. Agile software development teams provide repeatable results by adopting just the right amount of ceremony for the situation they face. (p. 6)*

Conforto, Amaral, da Silva, Di Felippo, and Kamikawachi (2016) analyzed 59 definitions covering the "agile" concept. They propose a comprehensive definition of the agility construct covering the entity, the event, the degree, the trigger, the purpose, and the circumstance as follows:

> *Agility is the project team's ability to quickly change the project plan as a response to customer or stakeholders [sic] needs, market or technology demands in order to achieve better project and product performance in an innovative and dynamic project environment. (p. 667)*

2.2 Benefits of Agile

Organizations might have very different reasons to implement agile. For example, their goal might be to improve quality, better respond to change, decrease lead time, release new product variants more often, reduce cost, or ensure that the product delivered corresponds better to what the customer wants (Kettunen & Laanti, 2008). Although many software developers could not imagine working any other way, surprisingly, very few studies have actually measured or demonstrated the benefits/improved performance due to agile. Many of the publications on agile are based on individual case studies or on observations by consultants implementing agile. Probably the most extensive study trying to assess the impact of implementing agile was performed at Nokia by Laanti, Salo, and Abrahamsson (2011). Their survey of more than 1,000 respondents in seven different countries in Europe, North America, and Asia reveals that:

> Most respondents agree on all accounts with the generally claimed benefits of agile methods. These benefits include higher satisfaction, a feeling of effectiveness, increased quality and transparency, increased autonomy and happiness, and earlier detection of defects. Finally, 60% of respondents would not like to return to the old way of working. (p. 276)

Although agile approaches have provided flexibility in the software development process, most benefits have been achieved within the Executing Process Group (Project Management Institute, 2012) of small projects composed of one or a few dedicated self-managed teams (Kruchten, 2013).

2.3 Agile and Traditional Project Management Approaches

Agile methodology is often presented in opposition to the more traditional project management principles and practice (Fernandez & Fernandez, 2008). For example, the *Agile Manifesto* (Agile Alliance, 2001) positions the four core values *over* the alleged traditional values. However, Kettunen (2009a) suggests that further improvements in software development could be inspired by organization-oriented business concepts, many of which are long-established project management concepts, such as concurrent engineering, multi-project management, being proactive, and so forth (Boehm, 2002; Boehm & Turner, 2003, 2004).

Al-Zoabi (2008) recommends a balanced combination of *plan-driven* traditional project management and an agile approach to manage projects, stating that the flexibility of an agile approach should be balanced with the advantage of a more traditional approach through a risk-based analysis. This is observed in a combination of XP and Prince2 (Al-Zoabi, 2008).

Anantatmula and Anantatmula (2008) show empirically that such a combined approach may be very valuable for the management of projects in an IT environment. It has also been shown that agile could be combined with stage gates in large organizations such as ABB, Ericsson, and Vodafone (Karlstrom & Runeson, 2005, 2006). This might lead to a different combination and alignment of the software development phases with the project management phases. However, this leads to a different perception of control between upper management (used to a more traditional gating approach) and the development teams:

> During the project, management was negative to the agile "method" used at the engineering level due to the fact that they felt uneasy with a different method. They felt less in control of the project and they missed the ability to squeeze extra functionality into the project without something else being removed. The developers[,] however, felt a strong sense of control in the project and were very pleased. The opinion was that the information that the management required existed, they just did not look in the right places. (p. 214)

Another option, according to Vinekar, Slinkman, and Nerur (2006), would be to have both the traditional and the agile approaches coexist in separate subunits within an ambidextrous organization, an approach referred to as

Bimodal IT (Gartner, 2016). The issue then becomes to develop criteria for selecting which approach to use on each project based on the advantages and disadvantages of each, for example, between the waterfall model, the V-Model, or agile (Balaji & Murugaiyan, 2012). Barlow et al. (2011) suggest a selection framework based on the volatility, the nature of the project interdependencies, and the project team size. Adoption of one agile methodology or the other would often be based on the organization's corporate culture and/or maturity (Gruver & Mouser, 2015; Iivari & Iivari, 2011).

2.4 Scaling Agility

Observing that agile is bringing benefits to small software development projects, many organizations are now attempting to apply the same principles but to larger projects. For this research project, it was important to clarify what was meant by *scaling* (i.e., what is considered a large project or a large organization when the time comes to use agile).

Ambler (2009) proposes a scaling model, called Agile Scaling Model (ASM), based on factors such as team size, geographical distribution, regulatory compliance, domain complexity, organizational distribution, technical complexity, organizational complexity, and enterprise discipline.

Kruchten (2013) also identifies eight scaling factors (system size, criticality, system age, rate of change, business model, stability of architecture, team distribution, and governance), which might distinguish the contexts in which agile would be easier to introduce than others. Based on this model, an *agile sweet spot* refers to:

> *The conditions under which most "labelled" agile software development have been developed, and for which success is pretty much assured. This would be the case for example of a web-based e-commerce site, built on dot-net technology by a small team, interacting with their customers. (p. 355)*

Table 2:   A Particular Context—The Agile Sweet Spot

System Size	Less than 15 person-months
Criticality	Simple, $ losses
System Age	Green field
Rate of Change	Medium or high
Business Model	In house
Architecture	Stable
Team Distribution	Colocated
Governance	Simple rules

This would translate into a context with particular characteristics. An example of a context corresponding to the agile sweet spot (Kruchten, 2013) is shown in Table 2.

In other words, while agile methodologies seem suited for small, colocated teams where the customer can be directly involved, there are a number of impediments to the scaling of these practices in large multisite, multi-customer, multi-project organizations; for example, the question of the customer representative or *product owner* is often problematic (Leffingwell, 2010; Lindvall et al., 2004).

The exact definition of agility scaling is not clear (Dingsøyr & Moe, 2014) but Dingsøyr, Fægri, and Itkonen (2014) suggest a taxonomy of scale of agile software development projects based on the number of teams where small scale corresponds to one team, large scale to two to nine teams, and very large scale to more than 10 teams. Using this scale, the qualitative portion of this research examines large-scale projects, and the survey examines both large-scale and very large-scale projects.

2.5 Examples of Using Agile at Scale

There has been limited research on the topic of implementing agile in large projects in large organizations

(Dyba & Dingsøyr, 2008; Razavi & Ahmad, 2014), although a number of specific cases have been investigated and documented. Grewal and Maurer (2007) studied the use of agile approaches in a medium-to-large-scale project in the oil industry over a period of two-and-a-half years. Gruver et al. (2013) published their experience of implementing agile in a large multisite project for a new series of printers at Hewlett-Packard, which subsequently led to a migration toward DevOps (Gruver & Mouser, 2015). The term DevOps is a derivative of development and operations, which is closely related to software engineering practices. DevOps has two components: an organizational change component that fosters improved collaboration among developers, testers, integrators and operators, and a technical component featuring automated testing, integration, deployment, and monitoring of the performance of systems in production (VersionOne, 2016). It is a more recent phenomenon within the family of agile techniques and is not the object of study in the present research.

Mahanti (2006) studied some of the challenges of introducing agile in organizations with four specific cases at ABB, Daimler-Chrysler, Motorola, and Nokia. He found that the primary challenge in adopting agile practices in large organizations was the integration of agile projects with the project environment's existing processes.

Fitzgerald, Stol, O'Sullivan, and O'Brien (2013) evaluated the applicability of agile methods for developing safety-critical systems in regulated environments and introduced the notion of continuous compliance and living traceability. Gat (2006) reported the large-scale deployment of agile software development in the Infrastructure Management Business Unit of BMC Software. Paasivaara, Durasiewicz, and Lassenius (2008a, 2008b) reported on a case study on agile practices in a 40-person development organization distributed between Norway and Malaysia. They also studied a large software development project of 20 teams distributed across four countries (Paasivaara & Lassenius, 2011). Goh, Pan, and Zuo (2013) investigated the processes of instilling agile IS (information systems) development practices in large-scale IT projects on the construction of the Beijing Capital International Airport Terminal 3 in preparation for the 2008 Olympic Games. Papadopoulos (2015) studied the transition from traditional to agile in a large global communications software and services company and saw a number of the agile benefits but also some important impediments to its implementation. Most of these case studies show that even though agile brings benefits when it is used in large projects, it is generally observed that adapting these practices in a large distributed setting is extremely challenging.

2.6 Scaling Frameworks

Some organizations have been trying to develop their own agile framework for use on large projects. However, a number of frameworks have been developed over time to facilitate the use of agile principles in larger projects. The most commonly used is Scaled Agile Framework (SAFe®), which has evolved from the Rational Unified Process (Leffingwell, 2015; Scaled Agile Framework, 2014). This has led to a SAFe® maturity model (Stojanov, Turetken, & Trienekens, 2015).

Other frameworks include Disciplined Agile Delivery (DAD) (Ambler & Lines, 2014; Disciplined Agile Delivery, 2015), Large-Scale Scrum (LeSS) (Larman, 2015; Larman & Vodde, 2013, 2014), and Nexus (Schwaber, 2015). All of these frameworks attempt to preserve the benefits of agile while improving the links to larger organizations.

Many of these frameworks link multiple agile projects in a program or a portfolio manager at the organizational level. Rautiainen, von Schantz, and Vahaniitty (2011) and Stettina and Hörz (2015) recently studied the consequences of managing large IT portfolios including agile projects.

2.7 Challenges of Scaling Up Agile

2.7.1 Organizational Aspects

Looking back at the agile principles (in Table 1), organizations implementing agile in large projects might wonder how to ensure that "business people and developers must work together daily throughout the project," or in large, complex systems to let "the best architectures, requirements, and designs emerge from self-organizing teams."

In fact, when trying to scale agile projects, organizational factors start to come into play, for example, elaborate organizational structures of the product owners and ScrumMasters, slower and less efficient decision making, and more complex collaboration and coordination (Highsmith, 2010; Papadopoulos, 2015). Conflicts might be observed when agile is introduced in organizations where traditional approaches are well established (Boehm & Turner, 2005), especially if it is only partly deployed (i.e., agile is not deployed in all the required functions of the organizations) (Laanti, 2012), or if it is combined with other processes (e.g., in new product development) (Kettunen, 2007).

2.7.2 Technical Aspects and Refactoring

Challenges might also be more technical. In large, complex systems, designing ahead, refactoring, maintaining continuous integration (and build process), automated testing, or testing with external systems might be very costly (Elshamy & Elssamadisy, 2007). In large projects, refactoring sometimes becomes a very expensive process:

> *Imagine a code base of a half million lines of code or more. A major refactoring to the code may take a month to be done. Some design ahead may be done to save expensive major refactoring later. Designing ahead has also its drawbacks as the design might not work for future requirements and then has to change or sometimes the design may be overkill to the requirements and will cause an overhead of maintaining extra complex*

code. There should be a compromise to make this decision of taking the chance of spending some time and effort of designing ahead for a design that might not work or may be more than what's really required for the project against spending time in refactoring existing code. (Elshamy & Elssamadisy, 2007, p. 50)

2.7.3 Organizational Culture

The relationship between organizational culture and the deployment of agile systems development has been investigated using the *competing values framework* (CVM) by (Iivari & Iivari, 2011). They tested 13 hypotheses justified by the four dimensions of organizational culture identified in the CVM. They report that "agile methods are most incompatible with the hierarchical culture orientation" (p. 517). Organizations with a relatively strong hierarchical culture will have a tendency to mix agile approaches with more formal methodologies: "This makes these combined models heavier and as a consequence they may start to lose some of their emergent agility" (p. 517). They found very interesting relationships between the organizational culture (e.g., development cultures or hierarchical cultures) and the enactment of the agile approaches:

Less mandatory methods may be more effectively enacted in organizations with a strong hierarchical culture than in organizations with a strong developmental culture, because the desired behavior will be followed more faithfully in the former case than in the latter case where we expect more method improvisation [. . .] Furthermore, one can conjecture that the more formalized an agile method becomes the sooner it will be considered dysfunctional in organizations with strong developmental culture. (p. 517)

2.7.4 Teams

The introduction of agile methods in large projects has very significant impacts on the organization of teams in projects.

Teams must be coordinated by establishing mechanisms, such as Scrum of Scrums (a regular meeting of the ScrumMasters that is usually attended by the project manager), architecture teams, project coordination teams, and product owner coordination teams. Elshamy and Elssamadisy (2007) summarize some of the communication challenges of having multiple teams:

> *One of the aspects common to many agile development (approaches) is that the entire team (business analysts, developers, and testers) collaborate very heavily. With a large project, this type of collaboration is difficult at best. What we have found again and again is that we tend to break up into subteams for better communication. The downside to subteams is the possibility that the subteams build stove-piped subsystems if communication is insufficient among the teams. Problems of consistency and duplication may go undiscovered. Of course, there are other practices that help alleviate these problems such as rotating team members among the subteams, having an overall design document, etc. [. . .] Another way to state this problem is that the different subteams may result in a non-homogeneous and inconsistent architecture. (p. 46)*

This issue gets even more dramatic when teams are spread over multiple sites, sometimes in multiple countries in different time zones. It becomes even worse when members of the same team are spread across multiple sites. Some of the fundamental principles related to open and frequent communication becomes a definite challenge. Teams must then implement facilitating technologies, such as videoconferencing, web cameras for daily Scrum meetings, frequent visits, unofficial distributed meetings, and annual gatherings (Paasivaara et al., 2008a, 2008b).

Spotify, for example, has started to establish innovative team structures for the company's 30 teams spread across three cities. They introduced the notion of *squads* (basic unit of development), *tribes* (a collection of squads that work in related areas), *chapters* (family of people having similar skills and working within the same general competency area, within the same tribe), and *guilds* (a more organic and wide-reaching "community of interest," a group of people who want to share knowledge, tools, code, and practices) (Kniberg & Ivarsson, 2012).

2.8 Summary of the Literature Review

A more recent publication by Dikert, Paasivaara, and Lassenius (2016) summarizes these challenges after surveying 52 publications describing 42 industrial cases presenting the process of taking large-scale agile development into use as follows:

- **Transformation challenges:** change resistance, skepticism toward the new way of working, top-down mandate creates resistance, and management unwilling to change;
- **Lack of investment:** lack of training, lack of coaching, too high workload, old commitments met, and need to rearrange space;
- **Difficult to implement:** misunderstanding agile concepts, lack of guidance from literature, agile customized poorly, reverting to old ways of working, and excessive enthusiasm;
- **Coordination challenges in multiteam environment:** difficulty interfacing among teams, challenging autonomous team model, global distribution challenges, and difficulty achieving technical consistency;
- **Different approaches emerge in a multiteam environment:** interpretation of agile differs among teams, and using old and new methods side by side;
- **Hierarchical management and organizational boundaries:** middle managers' new roles in agile unclear, management in waterfall mode, and internal silos kept;
- **Requirements engineering challenges:** high-level requirements management largely missing in agile,

requirements refinement challenging, difficulty in creating and estimating user stories, and gap between long- and short-term planning;

- **Quality assurance (QA) challenges:** accommodating nonfunctional testing, lack of automated testing, and requirements ambiguity affects QA; and
- **Integrating nondevelopment functions in the transformation:** other functions unwilling to change, challenges in adjusting to incremental delivery pace, challenges in adjusting product launch activities, and rewarding model not teamwork centric.

They also identified a number of success factors contributing to agile transformation, including management support, commitment to change, leadership, choosing and customizing the agile approach, piloting, training and coaching, engaging people, communication and transparency, mind-set and alignment, team autonomy, and requirements management.

In summary, the advantages of using agile approaches identified in the literature include a working environment that supports creativity and productivity, rapid adaptation to change, and value for the customer because of better identification of needs and priorities and faster multiple deliveries of functionalities. These advantages are more readily obtained in small, colocated teams working on small, noncritical, green field, in-house software projects with stable architectures and simple governance rules.

However, despite the development of some scaling frameworks, such as LeSS, DAD, or SAFe, little research has been published on the use of agile in large projects and large organizations. The next section describes the methodology that was used in this research to try to understand the challenges faced by these projects (and these organizations) and what they have tried to put in place to obtain the benefits of agile in this context.

CHAPTER 3

Methodology

Little is known about the subjects investigated in this research. For this reason, the study is exploratory. The research was conducted in two phases. In the first phase, qualitative case studies were conducted. The second phase was a survey to confirm and enrich the results of the case studies. The research can, therefore, be said to employ a mixed method (Tashakkori & Teddlie, 1998). A total of 48 substantially complete responses to the survey was received, which is too small to support most multivariate analyses. The results from the case studies and the survey are very consistent. In addition, the survey results quantify the trends observed in the case studies. The consistency between the results from the two phases is indicative of the generalizability of the results. Comparison with another recent survey by VersionOne (2016) (N=3,880) with several similar questions reveals that respondent demographics, the descriptions of the implementation of agile approaches, the benefits derived for the use of agile approaches, and the obstacles to implementation are very similar. The similarities indicate that the 48 responses to the survey in this research are representative of a larger population. Note that the survey in the present research contains several questions not included in the VersionOne survey. However, further research with larger sample sizes will be necessary to validate the generalizability of the results presented here.

3.1 The Qualitative Case Studies

Large organizations doing several large software projects were investigated. These types of organizations were chosen because they are ideal sites for exploring the use and impact of agile outside of the agile sweet spot at both project and organizational levels. One of the central features of agile is the presence of customer representatives in the role of product owner. This is also one of the features that are problematic in the application of agile in large organizations. For this reason, organizations with different types of relationships with customers were investigated. The customers vary on two important dimensions: number of customers and whether they were internal versus external customers.

Three case organizations were used to explore both the project and organizational levels of analysis. In each organization, interviews and analysis of documents were the primary sources of data. Interviews were conducted at both the organization level and the project level. The people targeted for organization-level interviews include members of senior management, program and portfolio managers, directors of project management offices, champions of agile, and line managers. The people targeted for project-level interviews include ScrumMasters, product owners, project managers, analysts, and system architects. An interview guide was prepared based on previous work (Petit & Besner, 2013), the literature review, and the research questions. The questions asked during the early part of the interview are open-ended. The interview guide provided a list of information to be collected during the interview, but not a list of questions to be asked directly, except as follow-up questions as the interview progresses. The interview guide was tested during several interviews and revised accordingly. Data relative to each level of analysis (project versus organization) were provided in many of the interviews.

The separation by level of analysis was, therefore, carried out during the analysis of the interviews. All interviews were recorded, transcribed, and analyzed using ATLAS.ti software. A total of 41 interviews with an average duration of one hour was conducted. The summary of interviewees is presented in Table 3.

The original research design called for the analysis of three projects composed of three or more development teams in each of three case study organizations. These were carried out in a company producing large, complex systems sold to outside customers, a financial services company, and a public organization. The analysis of the three case studies revealed a very high level of variability in the organizations' contexts and histories, in the organizational arrangements and role definitions that accompany the implementation of agile, and in the management practices put in place on each of the projects investigated. The analysis of

Table 3: Summary of Interviews for Nine Projects in Three Organizations

	Large System		Financial		Public		Total	
	Number of Interviews	Average Duration (Minutes)	Number of Interviews	Average Duration (Minutes)	Number of Interviews	Average Duration (Minutes)	Number of Interviews	Average Duration (Minutes)
Project Manager	5	65.6	2	64	3	79	10	69.3
ScrumMaster	2	41.5	5	66.6	4	52.3	11	56.8
Product Owner	1	68			3	61.7	4	63.3
Executive					3	44.7	3	44.7
PMO or Portfolio Manager	2	46.5	2	74.5			4	60.5
Analysts			1	56			1	56
Line Manager	1	66					1	66
Architect	1	49			6	52.7	7	52.1
Total / average	12	57.25	10	66.6	19	56.9	41	59.4

the three case studies provided a good understanding of these organizations. However, to what extent they were representative is unclear. For this reason, three additional 90-minute interviews were conducted with a key informant in three additional organizations. The three organizations were selected to be in industries similar to the initial cases (i.e., large system development, financial services, and public sector). The complementary interviews investigated the level of the organization and one specific large project, for an overall total of 12 projects. The interviews were again recorded, transcribed, and analyzed using ATLAS.ti. Because of the understanding of the context that emerged from the three original case studies, one interview with a key informant was sufficient for a good understanding of agile approaches to project management in the three additional organizations. There were many similarities and several significant differences among the six organizations investigated. The researchers decided that following the six case studies, the understanding of the use of agile methods on large software projects in large organizations was sufficient to adequately support the preparation of the survey for phase two.

3.2 The Survey Instrument

The survey instrument requested participation by practitioners able to provide a high-level description of a software development project with at least three development teams that was carried out in an organization with at least 2,000 employees. However, two responses with 1,600 and 1,652 employees, respectively, were retained in the sample. Three development teams are sufficient to produce coordination challenges not found with a single team. The minimum number of three development teams was based on the results of the analysis of the projects in the six organizations that participated in phase one and contact with Agile Montreal community of practice over several years showing that projects with significantly more than three development teams are relatively rare. Setting the minimum number of employees at 2,000 was somewhat arbitrary, but the researchers are aware that agile approaches are used primarily in small organizations and that setting the limit higher would make it difficult to gather sufficient survey data. An organization with 2,000 employees is large enough to have the effects of specialization and formalization that characterize large organizations (Mintzberg, 1979). A summary description of the Survey Questionnaire is provided in Table 4. The complete Survey Questionnaire can be found in the Appendix.

Table 4:   Survey Questionnaire (Overview)

Section 1. Respondent demographics

Section 2. The relevant organizational context:

a. Which in most cases is only a part of the organization, a division or subsidiary
b. The years when agile methods were used for the first time on small project and on large projects. From the case studies and a general knowledge of the context, it is known that many organizations, but not all, implement agile methods first on small projects
c. The level of maturity in the use of agile methods
d. The presence of an agile community of practice
e. The total number of projects and the proportion employing agile methods

Section 3. A specific large project that employed agile methods:

a. The level of knowledge of agile methods of people involved in this project
b. Type of deliverable, scope, and duration
c. Level of integration with other systems
d. Number and duration of sprints
e. Project organization:
    i. Number and composition of development teams
    ii. Other teams or committees
    iii. Other individuals
f. Project initiation, activities related to architecture and to the planning of sprints before the beginning of software development per se, often referred to as sprint zero
g. Agile practices employed
h. Benefits and disadvantages of agile methods and project performance

Section 4. The transition from traditional methods to agile methods:

From a general knowledge of the field, it is known that most large organizations had well-established traditional project management methods prior to implementing agile methods and that in most cases the two are present. However, some organizations use agile methods exclusively. For these reasons, Section 4 of the survey was completed only by respondents in contexts where both methods are currently in use.
a. Decision rules for determining which projects use agile methods
b. Performance objectives that motivated use of agile methods
c. Organizational objectives that motivated use of agile methods
d. Strategy for implementing agile methods, including change management
e. Organizational characteristics that supported implementation
f. Organizational characteristics that are obstacles to implementation
g. Performance outcomes
h. Organizational change outcomes
i. New and changed organizational roles, particularly for project managers, ScrumMasters, and product owners

3.3 Data Collection and Analysis

Invitations to participate in the survey were distributed through several channels. PMI provided logistic support for distribution. Invitations were also distributed through two decentralized international networks of groups dedicated to agile methods: http://at2015.agiletour.org and www.agilealliance.org. These communities organize annual conferences under the brand "Agile Tour," including the agile community of practice in the authors' home city of Montreal, who collaborated in this research. Invitations were also distributed using social media and the authors' personal networks. A total of 48 substantially complete responses to the survey was received. All of the case study organizations and the majority of the organizations of the survey respondents are using agile in contexts where traditional software project management methods are well established. However, a minority of survey respondents report on contexts in which all software development projects employ agile. Respondents in contexts in which both traditional methods and agile approaches are employed responded to the final section of the survey questionnaire. The objective of this section is to investigate the process by which agile approaches have been implemented into contexts dominated by traditional methods and to investigate how organizations allocate projects to traditional methods and agile approaches. This section of the survey also investigated the impact of the introduction of agile in organizations with well-established traditional methods. A total of 35 responses to this final section was received. The remaining 13 respondents or 27% are in contexts in which all projects are managed using agile.

The number of substantially complete responses is too small to support most multivariate analyses. However, the sample can support comparisons between responses to questions where this is relevant. Because there has been very little empirical research on this topic, the research is necessarily exploratory. There are no hypotheses to be tested, but the topic and the research questions imply that project and organizational size affect both the implementation and the use of agile. It is not possible to compare with organizations with fewer than 2,000 employees or with projects with fewer than three development teams, because these are excluded from the sample. However, it is possible to explore the effects of variations in organizational and project size within the sample. Mann–Whitney nonparametric t-tests are used to explore the effects of organizational size, project size, and development team size on all of the more than 250 variables in the survey (Sheskin, 2007). The measures of size are continuous variables that have been divided into almost equal groups around the median in order to evaluate their effect. The same technique is used to explore the effects of two dichotomous contextual variables: public versus private sector organizations and projects to update existing systems versus projects to develop new systems.

The survey contains questions that evaluate the knowledge of agile and the support for the implementation of agile among different groups within the organization. Because there are several groups, the analysis of these questions requires paired comparisons of means, which is carried out using the Wilcoxon Technique (Sheskin, 2007).

3.4 The Case Study Organizations

The mandate of all the projects is to develop and/or make significant changes to large, complex systems with multiple interconnections to adjacent systems. All six organizations have introduced agile into a context where well-established traditional project management methods are in place.

The two financial services companies in this study have formalized structures and procedures and a high degree of specialization. The business processes in this type of organization make extensive use of complex computer systems that are interconnected internally and with other organizations, including customer organizations and suppliers of information. The software projects are all related to the development and/or updating of systems that are used by operational employees of the company, by employees in other organizations that are connected to their systems, and by online customers. With these types of end users, it is relatively easy to identify which organizational units are the customers from which the product owners can be drawn. However, as stated in the literature, and as is shown in the results of this research, the role of product owner is problematic. Financial services is an important sector in which large-scale agile projects are found; 26% of the respondents to the survey are from this sector, and it is the second most common industry after software reported in the VersionOne (2016) survey.

The two companies that produce large, complex systems that are sold to other organizations for use in their internal business processes have very different relationships with their end users. The product is used by multiple independent customer organizations, which are often in competition with one another. In addition, the contractual process through which the product is sold often specifies what is to be delivered in rather precise detail. This introduces rigidities that are difficult to reconcile with the flexibility of agile approaches and the idea of updating and reprioritizing the product backlog continuously. In these two companies, the product owner role is filled by product managers, who have the authority and the interest to direct product development.

The systems in the two public sector organizations are numerous, large, interconnected internally, and interconnected with other organizations, many of which are also in the public sector, but not all. The information technologies in these two organizations are very different. One has many large legacy systems based on outdated technology that are performing rather poorly. The tight integration of the systems, the specialization of both people and organizational units, and the activities to integrate and test all changes before the infrequent releases into production all create obstacles to the use of agile. The organization has a plan to update its databases and systems with a view to making them less tightly integrated and more amenable to more frequent releases.

The other public sector organization has up-to-date technology. The part of the organization that was investigated is responsible for a central data bus (i.e., a shared communication channel facilitating communication between software modules). The end users are internal to the organization. The challenge in this organization is to respond more quickly and more adequately to priority system development requests.

CHAPTER 4

Results

4.1 Characteristics of Respondents, Their Organizations, and Their Projects

The following subsections present the characteristics of survey respondents, their organizations, and their projects. The objective of these sections is to provide information on the context of the survey and information relative to the generalizability of the results.

4.1.1 Respondent Demographics

- 44 years old
- 31% female
- 5.6 years of experience with agile
- Well educated (40% undergraduate degree, 58% graduate degree)

The respondents' primary roles in the project are presented in Table 5, with the number of respondents indicated:

Table 5:   The Respondents' Primary Roles

Program manager	12
Manager (IT)	7
Project manager	6
ScrumMaster	6
Agile coach	4
Manager (business or product unit)	3
Portfolio manager	3
Product owner (PO)	2
Business analyst	2
Manager (other)	1
Technical lead	1
Technical owner	1

4.1.2 Countries of Users and Producers of Software

Two phenomena make the identification of the county of residence of both users and producers complex and fastidious: (1) many organizations outsource the production of software to developers in other countries, referred to as "offshoring," and (2) many organizations produce software for the international market. All but one of the 48 survey respondents identify the country in which the majority of developers reside. But only 36 identify the country of residence of the users. It is assumed that these respondents are producing software for an international market. Table 6 presents the portrait of responses to these two questions. Because the sample is small, the distribution presented in the table is not representative. However, it provides an illustration of the diversity in the geographic locations of users and developers. For example, India is a common destination

Table 6: Geographic Distribution of Users and Developers

Development and users in same country	US (11), Canada (10), UK, Sweden, India, Ireland, and Belgium (1 each)	26
Development offshored from	US (4), UK, Canada, Hong Kong, Brazil, Australia, and France (1 each)	10
Development offshored to	India (3), Hong Kong (2), Canada, Ireland, Chile, Germany, and China (1 each)	10
Developing for international markets	Canada (6), India (2), US, Spain, and Netherlands (1 each)	11

of offshore development, but also develops software for both international and domestic markets and Hong Kong is both an offshore developer and a country that has development done offshore. In addition, industrialized countries such as Germany and Canada receive mandates to develop software for specific foreign markets; this typically takes place within multinational firms.

4.1.3 Description of the Organizational Context—Private and Public Sectors

The survey sample is split almost evenly between private (52%) and public sector organizations. Of the more than 250 variables in the survey, only 10 significant differences at the level of $p \leq 0.05$ are observed. There are more female respondents from public sector organizations, 52% compared with 12% ($p \leq 0.003$). The public sector projects are bigger; 114 people on average work on public sector projects at their peak, compared to 74 people in the private sector ($p \leq 0.050$). An examination of the effects of project size reveals that none of the significant differences between public and private organizations is attributable to differences in project size.

Both private and public organizations do equal numbers of update and new system projects. However, among those reporting on update projects, the private sector organizations maintain more versions of the system, 3.5 on average, compared to 2.3 for those in the public sector ($p \leq 0.043$). This difference between private and public sector organizations is not explained by differences in the types of projects being undertaken (internal versus external users and/or customers). Private organizations fill their product owner (PO) roles more often with people from business analysis ($p \leq 0.020$), while POs in public organizations come more often from among the operational personnel of the customer organization ($p \leq 0.003$). It is not clear what these differences are attributable to. POs in private organizations also come more often from product management and marketing roles, roles that are uncommon in public organizations.

The agile practices and techniques used in both types of organizations are almost identical. The only significant difference is the greater use of test-driven development in the public sector ($p \leq 0.030$). Survey respondents identified the organizational roles that were affected by the implementation of agile. The only significant difference is that public sector organizations identify the tester role more often ($p \leq 0.029$). These two results are consistent. The differences related to testing may be related to the state of the testing environments of public and private organizations, however; the authors do not have access to comparisons between the two. This may be an opportunity for future research.

The survey instrument presents a list of possible benefits of the use of agile and respondents choose which are relevant to the project they describe. The responses can be analyzed in two ways. The frequency of responses can be rank ordered to identify the most and least often cited and the sequences of public and private organizations can be compared. An alternative approach is to assess whether the frequencies of responses to a specific benefit between public and private organizations are significantly different using Mann–Whitney nonparametric t-tests. Both approaches are used. However, the analysis of rank order is not easily supported by statistical techniques. The p-values reported are therefore from this second measure. On both of these measures, the importance of both being more centered on the creation of business value ($p \leq 0.029$) and producing code of better quality ($p \leq 0.050$) are greater in public organizations. Lower development costs is ranked ninth of 11 benefits in both public and private organizations, but is mentioned significantly more often in public organizations (p ≤ 0.041). Survey respondents from both the public and the private sectors indicate that the agile project they describe is more successful than traditional projects in their organization, which is not surprising. What is noteworthy is that respondents in public organizations report a significantly greater improvement over traditional projects (p ≤ 0.037). This portrait corresponds with one of the public sector case study organizations in which the poor quality of their legacy systems, the inefficiency of their development efforts, and the poor contribution of their legacy systems to business objectives are the primary justifications for radical change and implementation of agile. The results presented here may indicate that a significant number of public organizations are in this situation, but caution should be exercised because of the small sample size. This is again a subject for future research.

4.1.4 Description of the Organizational Context— Organization Size

The survey instructions requested responses relative to organizations with at least 2,000 employees. However, two responses with 1,600 and 1,652 employees, respectively, were retained in the sample. The average number of employees in the entire organization is 42,212. The organizations in the survey sample varied a great deal in size, up to 180,000 employees. Of the more than 250 variables in the survey, the organization size has a significant effect on only a very small number. This can be interpreted to mean that the implementation of agile in organizations with only a few thousand employees and with tens of thousands of employees has quite similar effects. It is plausible that the effects of organization size of the specialization of human resources and the formalization of organizational processes are largely present in organizations with only a few thousand employees and that their effects on agile implementation are not significantly different from those in much larger organizations. The case studies and the survey instrument reveal that the relevant organizational context is not the entire organization, even in the case of organizations with a few thousand employees. This may also explain, at least in part, why there are so few significant differences.

The significant differences between larger and smaller organizations in the sample are as follows:

- Larger organizations have a longer experience with the use of agile on large projects, 1.7 years more on average ($p \leq 0.013$).
- POs in larger organizations are more knowledgeable about agile ($p \leq 0.038$).
- Larger organizations have business analysts and tech leads as individual members of the project organizations more often ($p \leq 0.040$ for both).
- Development teams on projects in larger organizations are not more likely to be in the same time zone, but those that are, are more likely to be within one kilometer of each other. This may be because very large organizations often have facilities that house large numbers of employees.
- Smaller organizations report significantly more improvement in the quality of the code with agile approaches ($p \leq 0.013$).

A distinction is made between the entire organization and the part of the organization the respondent considers relevant to the specific project he or she describes. The entire organization is the relevant context for the description of only 21% of the projects described by respondents. For the other 79% of projects described, the relevant context is a small part of the entire organization, the average number of employees of which is 2,068. The size of the relevant organizations varied a great deal—from 50 to 20,000 people. From the interviews and from an examination of the survey responses it is clear that in some cases what the respondents consider the relevant organization is limited to the part of the organization that actually produces the system, while others extend it to include all the employees in the parts of the organization that will use or be affected by the use of the system being produced. The differences in possible interpretations of the question related to the size of the relevant part of the organization render the interpretation difficult.

4.1.5 Description of the Organizational Context—Primary Activity

The primary activity of the relevant part of the organization is presented in Table 7.

Table 7: Primary Activity of the Organization

Financial services	11
Information technology	7
Telecommunications	7
Software development	7
Government	3
Manufacturing	2
New product development	2
Health services	2
Transportation and logistics	2
Engineering	1
Construction	1
Training/education	1
Agriculture	1
Consulting (other than engineering or IT)	1

4.1.6 Description of the Organizational Context—Use of Agile Approach

On average, 98 projects are under way at the same time in the organization. Twenty-seven percent of organizations report using agile on all their projects. In the other organizations, as low as 9% of projects employ agile approaches. The 35 responses from organizations that use both agile and traditional approaches methods are examined further, in Section 4 of the survey.

Table 8: The Organizational Structure

Functional	16%
Weak matrix	29%
Balanced matrix	40%
Strong matrix	10%
By project	2%

Agile approaches have been in use for an average of five years within the organizations and for an average of three years on large projects. A total of 54% of organizations has an agile community of practice and those that do have had one for three years on the average. The respondents consider their organizations to be quite mature in the use of agile; on a capability maturity model integration (CMMI)-inspired scale, the average level of maturity is 2.8. The structure of the organization close to the project is presented in Table 8.

4.1.7 Description of the Specific Projects

Survey respondents describe a specific large project employing agile that has been completed or is close to completion. This research investigates the effect of the use of agile on projects with three development teams or more. The case study projects are much more homogeneous; the projects in the case study organizations have durations of approximately two years, while projects in the survey vary a great deal, with durations from 10 weeks to 6.5 years, with an average of 1.6 years. The survey employs two measures of project size: number of development teams, which varies from three to 45, and the peak number of project participants or staff, with an average of 94 and a maximum value of 700. Projects with large staff are also of longer duration. Table 9 presents the significant differences between larger and smaller projects as measured by both staff size and number of development teams. The numbers in the table are the level of significance of the difference or p-value.

Table 9:   Effects of Project Size

	Staff Size	# Development Teams
Development team members colocated	0.001	0.000
Development team size	0.031	
Program manager on project	0.028	
Agile knowledge of development teams		0.031
Agile coach on development team		0.018
PO on development team		0.046
Tester on development team		0.048
Number of releases		0.046
Number of sprints before integration	0.057	
Number of sprints per release	0.031	
Number of update versions		0.023
Performance goal to lower development costs	0.006	
Higher development costs	0.034	
Support of cultural value of autonomy	0.044	
Organizational change goal servant leadership	0.037	

Both measures of project size are associated with development team members being more often colocated. This is the only effect of size common to both measures. There are significant differences in project organizations. Larger projects as measured by staff size have bigger development teams and are more likely to have a program manager in the project organization. Larger projects as measured by the number of development teams with team members who are more knowledgeable of agile are more likely to have an agile coach, a PO, and/or a tester on each development team. The way the content of the project deliverable is structured during development is different as well. Large projects as measured by staff size have more sprints before integration and release. Larger projects as measured by the number of development teams have more releases.

In update projects, larger projects as measured by the number of development teams maintain more versions. Larger projects as measured by staff size seem to have issues with the cost of development, which is higher despite the fact that lowering this cost is a performance goal. Larger projects as measured by staff size also have issues related to organizational culture. They report that having a culture that values autonomy is more important for implementation and that a change from a command and control leadership style to one of servant leadership is a specific organizational change objective. Several of these effects have face validity. For example, it is not surprising that bigger projects are of longer duration and have bigger development teams, more specialized human resources, more releases, more versions, more sprints before integration and release, and higher development cost, which may be attributable to the difficulties of coordinating larger development projects. Thus, there are some effects of project size beyond the level of three development teams. The fact that project size beyond three development teams does not have a significant effect on any of the other variables indicates that the description of agile development presented in this report is relevant to most large projects.

The vast majority of systems under development are integrated with other systems, an average of 10.7 other systems. Only two survey respondents report that their system is a standalone. In 49% of the responses, the systems have a hardware component; this incudes projects that purchase and install equipment such as servers. The types of deliverables are presented in Table 10. None of the projects in the sample have deliverables

Table 10:   Types of Project Deliverables

Used primarily by employees of the organization	21%
Used primarily by online customers of the organization	32%
Used as much by employees as by online customers of the organization	26%
Sold to organizations for use in their internal systems	21%

that are sold to individuals, such as software for income taxes, pacemakers, or videogames. This is a limit of this study.

The deliverables are divided evenly between updates of an existing system or product (54%) and development of new systems or products. When the deliverable is an update, the number of versions that are maintained at the same time is important, particularly for those that sell their product to multiple customers. The respondents report that for system updates, an average of 2.9 versions are maintained in parallel, including the one under development. A systematic comparison between update and new system projects reveals that they are remarkably similar. Of the more than 250 variables in the survey, significant differences are observed on only three variables. In approximately 25% of cases, both update and new system projects have two project managers, one from IT and one from the customer organization. However, the number of new system projects that have a single project manager is significantly greater ($p \leq 0.029$). Several of the update projects have multiple project managers for different components or domains. New system projects have significantly more releases ($p \leq 0.021$). An organizational culture that includes the right to make mistakes is included among the organizational characteristics that support the implementation of agile significantly more often on update projects ($p \leq 0.048$). The point here is not so much the details of the small number of significant differences. The point is rather that very few significant differences are found and that the results of this research can likely be applied to both update and new system projects.

4.2 Implementation of Agile Approaches

4.2.1 Motives for Implementing Agile Approaches

The literature on agile claims that these approaches provide many performance advantages when compared to traditional methods. The performance motives that justified the decision to use agile identified in the interviews and in the survey are largely the same as those reported in the agile literature. In interviews and in the

Table 11:   Anticipated and Realized Performance Benefits of Agile

Better adapted to customer needs	71%
Better prioritization	67%
More centered on the creation of business value	62%
More rapid delivery to customers	62%
Development of fewer features that are never used	39%
Code of better quality	34%
Lower development costs	26%
Lower operating costs	19%
Documentation that is better adapted	11%

survey, respondents report that the performance objectives are met. The performance benefits of agile as reported in the survey are presented in Table 11 in decreasing order of mention.

In addition to the performance objectives often referred to in the literature, organizations are pursuing organizational change objectives as well. Interviewees and survey respondents report that the organizational change objectives listed in Table 12 are used to justify the use of agile and are realized during implementation in similar proportions. There is, however,

Table 12:   Organizational Change Objectives

Improved collaboration among development teams	59%
Better communication and understanding between developers and end users	55%
Better collaboration among organizational units	50%
Improved satisfaction of personnel	44%
Empowerment of personnel	39%
Improved software engineering practices	37%
Better organizational climate	35%
Increased motivation and commitment of personnel	33%
Change from command and control to servant leadership	26%

one exception: "better communication and understanding be-tween developers and end users" is an unexpected organizational change benefit for 21% of respondents. It is an objective for 39% of survey respondents, but a realized benefit of implementing agile for 70% of respondents (the 55% reported below is the aver-age of the two responses). The organizational change objectives are presented in decreasing order of mention in Table 12.

Note that in some of the case study organizations and in the survey data, improved software engineering practices are one of the organizational change objectives. This is the case where the poor performance of traditional methods is one of the jus-tifications for using agile. Software engineering practices are only indirectly related to agile. However, the agile principle that "Continuous attention to technical excellence and good design enhances agility" (Agile Alliance, 2001) can be seen to imply a link between software engineering excellence and agile approaches. It is reasonable to assume that the improved software engineering practices are at least in part responsible for the performance im-provements associated with the change. In these situations, agile approaches seem to benefit from performance improvements that are at least in part attributable to improvements in soft-ware engineering practices that could have been implemented without the implementation of agile. It is plausible that the mo-mentum of the change to agile approaches with significant sup-port from upper management makes improvements in software engineering practices easier to implement. It is also plausible that the frequent integration, tests, and demos create an environment that fosters improvements in the quality of the code.

In several of the case studies, the change to agile approaches is motivated in part by the demands of young qualified software de-velopers. In labor markets where the demand for qualified devel-opers exceeds the supply, these workers can be seen as volunteer labor in that they can choose the place where they work. In these situations, being able to provide a suitable working environment may provide organizations with a competitive advantage in that they are more able to recruit and retain qualified personnel. To a lesser extent, a change from command and control leadership style to servant leadership (Greenleaf, 2002) is also reported, which may also be related to the provision of a working climate better adapted to this type of personnel.

4.2.2 Disadvantages of Agile Approaches

Despite the hype in the agile literature, there are drawbacks to the use of agile. Several were reported in the case studies, which formed the bases of a survey question on the issue. The frequency of mention of disadvantages is presented in Table 13.

Some of the disadvantages reported are the exact opposite of benefits reported in Table 11. These include higher development costs, code of lower quality, and higher operating costs. Note that these are the three disadvantages least often mentioned. This indicates that the use of agile does not always produce the benefits with which it is often associated. In a minority of cases, the impact is the exact opposite. This begs the question as to what conditions foster the implementation of agile approaches and the generation of the benefits with which agile is often associated—an issue addressed in the following section.

The five most frequently mentioned disadvantages are all issues that are addressed in the literature and in the case study interviews. The difficulty in committing to project parameters is related to project approval processes that require that the detailed scope of the project and project plan be submitted for

Table 13: Disadvantages of Agile

Difficulty in committing to project parameters	58%
Creation of technical debt	49%
Documentation of poorer quality	42%
More refactoring	40%
Architecture more poorly structured	26%
Higher development costs	16%
Code of lower quality	14%
Higher operating costs	5%

approval before the project can be initiated, which is a common feature of traditional project approval and project portfolio management processes. There is a conflict here between a project management culture, which requires that the project parameters be determined in detail in advance, and the agile approach of progressive definition. In many large organizations dominated by traditional project management methods, the conflict is very difficult to resolve. The effect is often that projects are managed with a waterfall approach that is contrary to agile principles.

The focus on immediate delivery and results and the focus on features rather than components that are at the heart of the agile philosophy can lead to a short-term view that neglects issues of technical debt. The choice to develop features that produce short-term value can lead the development of solutions that will need to be reworked later when other more complex features are developed. This leads to more refactoring.

The *Agile Manifesto* values "working software over comprehensive documentation" (Agile Alliance, 2001). This has led to poor documentation in many situations, 42% of responses here. Some interviewees argue that this is a misinterpretation of the *Agile Manifesto*. They say that traditional documentation is too detailed, too cumbersome, and inaccurate, and therefore, is not used very extensively. They argue that documentation should be lighter and better adapted to use after it is produced. Note that 11% of respondents report that documentation is better adapted with agile. If this is representative of the reality of agile software development, there are many more cases of poor documentation than there are of documentation that is lighter and better adapted. Note that quality of the documentation is less visible during testing, integration, and demos than other features of the deliverables and may not receive as much attention.

The issues of technical debt and of refactoring are related to the issue of architecture that is more poorly structured, which in turn is related to the agile principle that "The best architectures, requirements, and designs emerge from self-organizing teams" (Agile Alliance, 2001). This issue is addressed in the section on system architecture and front-end planning.

4.2.3 Conditions That Foster and Hinder the Implementation of Agile

The analysis of the case studies reveals that many organizational conditions either foster or hinder the implementation of agile. These formed the bases for survey questions on these issues. Table 15 presents the organizational characteristics that support the implementation of agile, while Table 14 presents the obstacles to implementation. The items in the tables are based on an analysis of the case study interviews. Many of the items in the list of obstacles are the same as those in the list of characteristics that support implementation but expressed negatively. However, in some cases the items mentioned frequently as obstacles are different. For this reason, both lists are presented here. An "X" in the right-hand column of Table 15 indicates that the item is an obstacle in some organizations, as shown in Table 14, and a characteristic that supports implementation of agile in other organizations. This is an illustration of the variability in organizational contexts.

Not surprisingly, management support is the most prevalent characteristic. Management support has long been known as a critical factor in any organizational change efforts (Young & Poon, 2013). The level of support for implementation of agile by different people in different roles is evaluated in the survey on a 7-point Likert scale. The scores are reported in Table 16.

Table 14:   Organizational Characteristics That Are Obstacles

A command and control management style	77%
Project approval processes that require the project parameters be well defined in advance	65%
Lack of understanding of agile approach	65%
Role definitions that are not aligned with agile methodologies	65%
An organizational culture that values detailed processes	48%
An organizational culture that values standardized processes	45%
Lack of adhesion of middle managers	42%
The desire of personnel to work with traditional methods	32%
Lack of adhesion of project managers	23%

Table 15: Organizational Characteristics That Support Implementation

Management support	67%	X
Personnel that wish to work using agile approach	58%	X
Acceptance by the IT department	52%	
An organizational culture that values flexibility	52%	X
An organizational culture that values transparency	39%	
An organizational culture that values objective measures of performance	36%	
Poor performance of traditional projects	33%	
Acceptance by the client	33%	
An organizational culture that values autonomy	30%	X
Availability of human and financial resources to support the implementation	27%	
A good understanding of agile methodologies by all participants	24%	X
An organizational culture that includes the right to make mistakes	21%	
An organizational culture that values delegation	18%	

The results presented are consistent with the content of interviews from the case studies, during which support by these groups of managers, or the lack thereof, is mentioned very often. Note also that acceptance by the IT department is the third most frequently mentioned condition facilitating implementation. Acceptance by the client is also mentioned by 11% of respondents. Acceptance by the IT department and by the client is certainly related to their provision of support.

Table 16: The Level of Support of People in Different Roles

Project personnel	5.18
Management of IT	4.34
Upper management	4.24
Business unit managers	4.11

Pair-wise comparisons using the Wilcoxon technique reveal that only the differences between the support of project personnel and all the other groups are significant ($p \leq 0.007$). Note that having personnel who wish to work using agile is the second most frequently mentioned organizational characteristic that supports implementation of agile. This is mentioned very often as a driving force for implementing agile and for choosing the specific contexts in which it is implemented; see Section 4.2.5 on the agile sweet spot for further discussion. Situations vary from one organization to the next; however, note that the desire of personnel to work with traditional methods is also mentioned as an obstacle. Both adhesion of and resistance from development personnel are present in the case studies. In some cases, pressure from young and highly qualified developers is a driving force for implementation of agile. In other cases, or with other groups in the same organization, familiarity with and faith in traditional methods and traditional role definitions are significant sources of resistance to change. The new role definitions can be a threat to some, particularly programmers who are comfortable becoming programmer/analysts or developers; see Section 4.4.2 on new and modified organizational roles.

The list of obstacles includes the lack of adhesion of two groups—middle managers and project managers—as well as role definitions that are not aligned with agile. With semiautonomous development teams and POs making decisions about priorities, middle managers and project managers can get "stuck in the middle," so to speak. In many organizations that have the adhesion of both upper management and development personnel, the middle managers and/or project managers can be obstacles, particularly where their roles are either not defined in the agile approaches or are in conflict with them; see Section 4.4.5 on the role of project managers.

The importance of organizational culture is mentioned frequently in the literature on agile (Iivari & Iivari, 2011; McAvoy & Butler, 2009; Misra, Kumar, & Kumar, 2009; Sheffield & Lemétayer, 2013). Several of the organizational characteristics that foster implementation are related to organizational culture.

These include valuing flexibility, autonomy, delegation, and transparency, which are central to the agile philosophy. An organizational culture that includes the right to make mistakes is important because the agile approach incites people to experiment, to measure the results, and to change—often in a continuous improvement effort. The importance of cultures that value objective measures of performance is related to calls to implement agile with the goal of providing measurable and meaningful business value rather than just following the fad (Gruver & Mouser, 2015). There were numerous references to measurable improvements in the interviews as well. Culture and process are related. Traditional organizations and traditional project management value detailed and standardized processes and a command and control management style. Both are also associated with project approval processes that require the project parameters be well defined in advance. Together these form important obstacles to the implementation of agile.

In the case study interviews, the implementation of agile is justified very often by reference to the poor performance of traditional software project management practices. In as least one case study, this is the primary and the official justification.

An understanding of agile, or lack thereof, has important impacts on implementation. The knowledge of agile of people in different roles, as assessed on a 7-point Likert scale, is shown Table 17. There are approximately three groups: at one extreme, project managers and development teams with significantly more knowledge of agile, at the other extreme upper management with significantly less, and with the remaining three in between. With six groups, pair-wise comparisons are a bit fastidious. Analysis showed that several of these differences are significant. The situation varies enormously from one organization to the next: Upper management scores range from 1 to 5 and project management's range from 1 to 7, on the 7-point scale. A lack of knowledge in any of these groups can be an obstacle to implementation. Because the support of upper management is almost a necessary condition for any organizational change, a lack of understanding of agile can severely limit possibilities for

Table 17:   Knowledge of Agile of Different Groups

Project managers	4.1
Development teams	4.0
IT management	3.6
Product owners	3.5
Business unit or product managers	3.1
Upper management	2.6

their implementation. The understanding of agile by those who are actively involved in system development is obviously critical. The fact that many product owners have limited understanding of agile is problematic; see Section 4.4.3 on this role. A lack of knowledge on the part of IT and business unit and product managers can lead to a lack of support (see Table 17). Note that many of these managers are in the middle management positions referred to above, which can be sources of resistance to change.

The availability of human and financial resources to support the implementation is a critical success factor of any organizational change. However, resources are often not made available to support change. Survey respondents report that the extent to which the implementation was accompanied by resources for organizational change management—including training, coaches, and change agents—was less than moderate, an average of 3.8 on a 7-point Likert scale. However, there is a great deal of variability in the level of resourcing of change efforts; responses varied from 1 to 7 on the 7-point scale.

4.2.4 Implementation Strategies

The implementation strategies of all six case study organizations and of 74% of the organizations of survey respondents started with pilot projects. For an analysis of the characteristics of projects selected for the implementation, see Section 4.2.5 on the agile sweet spot. All of the development teams in the case studies and one third of teams in the survey have agile coaches. It is not clear why organizations in the survey choose to have agile coaches or not. It is not related to the number of years the organization has been using agile or the level of maturity in agile. The role of the agile coaches was primarily to support the implementation of Scrum methods on development teams. However, the implementation strategies have very little else in common. The extent to which agile has become well established in the six case study organizations varies a great deal. The six organizations are presented in approximately decreasing order of the extent to which agile is well established.

One of the organizations experimented with agile on small projects in one department from 2007 to 2009 and deployed these approaches on all of their software development projects between 2010 and 2013. Agile is now well established throughout the firm on both large and small software development projects. The other five organizations are in early stages of implementation, particularly for large projects. A second organization has been using agile on small projects for five years and has just completed one large and very successful project using agile approaches. Agile is well on the way to becoming well established for both large and small projects in this organization. A third organization is the IT department of a public organization composed of approximately 250 people, where agile was introduced following years of unsuccessful projects using traditional methods. This is the only case study that uses a scaling framework, a mixture of Nexus and LeSS. Their ambition is to gradually move away from project development to more continuous deliveries using a data bus structure. In a fourth organization, agile is currently being applied for the first time on pilot projects. The implementation is being sponsored by the CEO and the board of directors in response to an external audit that showed that the organization's software development projects and its legacy systems are performing very poorly. A new vice president and a new senior manager have been brought in to manage the implementation process. Contrary to the recommendation in the literature (Kruchten, 2013) and the practice in most of the other organizations, they have selected large projects as the pilots for implementation. The strategy is to show that agile can be applied to large projects and to demonstrate top management commitment to large-scale conversion to agile. At the time of the interviews, the pilot projects had been under way for two years. The pilot projects are well along the learning curve that accompanies the change in organization and in methods and several indicators show that the performance of the pilot projects is meeting expectations. It seems likely that top management will continue to support the large-scale conversion to agile in this organization. The fifth organization implemented agile on one large project between 2008 and 2012. This organization is a small R&D and product development unit of a large multinational firm. The project was very successful and might have led to further use of agile approaches in this unit, but due to an unrelated reorganization of the multinational firm, several small R&D units were closed, including this one. It is not possible to know what impact this experiment has had, if any. In the final organization, several small projects have been done using agile since 2005. The early pilots were the result of local and personal initiatives. Initially, a set of rules was used to determine whether to use agile approaches or traditional methods. However, these rules were not formalized, and at the time of the interviews the document containing the rules could not be located. In 2007, the CIO declared that all software development projects should use agile, but the resistance from the personnel in the IT department resulted in only a limited number of projects using agile. Agile approaches were only used when a champion of these approaches was on the team. People on other teams said that "agile approaches are flexible, so we will be flexible and change methodologies to our liking." Because they preferred traditional methods, there was little change. Many projects did analysis sprints, followed by development sprints, which were followed in turn by integration and test sprints. After a long series of sprints, a product could be demonstrated to customers and potentially released. In 2013, a new CIO put an end to the use of agile and returned to traditional methods. The case study projects in this organization were all initiated in the period prior to 2013. In the period following the interviews, a new CIO has started to support local initiatives to use agile, in part because of the poor performance of traditional methods.

It is difficult to draw conclusions from a small sample, however; implementation in only one of the six organizations relied almost entirely upon initiatives by local champions, and this implementation has been unsuccessful over an extended period of time. The survey results also show that bottom-up implementation strategies are used infrequently (14% of responses). This implementation strategy might not lead to large-scale deployment, as shown by the final case study. The infrequent use of bottom-up implementation strategies and the failure in this one case study are consistent with the importance of management support for implementation, as noted in Section 4.2.3 on conditions fostering implementation. The survey results also indicate considerable variability; 33% of organizations implemented agile on large and small projects the same year, while the remaining organizations used agile on small project for up to nine years before implementing on large projects. The survey results also show a great deal of variety in the proportion of projects using agile in the organization—from 9% to 100%, with an average of 55%. It is clear that both the strategies for implementing agile and the success of implementation vary a great deal.

4.2.5 The Agile Sweet Spot

The fact that most organizations use agile on some projects but not all brings up the question of what the characteristics of projects selected for the use of agile are. Kruchten (2013) identifies the conditions under which agile approaches are easier to implement and produce better results more consistently, as shown in Table 2. In several of the case study organizations, choices are being made as to which projects employ agile and which do not. During the interviews in these organizations, respondents were asked to identify the characteristics used to select projects for agile approaches. None of these organizations had a clear policy regarding which projects should be done using agile approaches or traditional methods. The survey results report that only 23% of organizations using both agile approaches and traditional methods have a clear policy. It seems that in many cases, the choice to use agile is influenced to a considerable extent by the personal preferences of managers and of project personnel.

A total of 27 survey respondents came from contexts where both agile approaches and traditional methods identify the characteristics of the projects done using agile. Some identify only a few characteristics, while others identify a large number. The distribution of responses is presented in Table 18.

It should be remembered that in many organizations agile approaches are not yet well established and that organizations are choosing contexts where they are more likely to be accepted and to succeed. The criteria used to select projects for use of an agile approach presented in Table 18 have been divided into

Table 18:   Criteria Used to Select Projects for Use of Agile Approach

Client acceptance of agile methods	54%
Human resources	
Wish of personnel to use agile methods	42%
Human resources available full-time	23%
Technical competency	23%
Capacity of people to fill multiple roles	23%
Capacity of people to work on teams	19%
Human resources that are geographically close	15%
Project characteristics	
New systems	35%
High rate of change	35%
Small projects	31%
Independent of other systems in the organization	27%
Simple projects	23%
Decomposable projects	23%
Stable architecture	15%
Projects that involve only one organizational unit	15%
Simple governance rules	8%

three groups. The project characteristics are those identified by Kruchten (2013). Table 18 identifies two additional sets of criteria: client acceptance of agile approaches and the characteristics of availability human resources. Note that client acceptance is the most important criterion.

4.2.6 Integration with Other Systems

A prominent feature of the case study interviews is the frequent mention of issues related to the integration of the system being developed or modified with many other systems within the organization and with systems external to the organization. Likewise, survey respondents report that their projects are integrated with an average of 10.7 other systems. Interviewees report that the integration with other systems prevents the frequent deliveries of software features to users because of the integration and testing required and because of organizational policies that limited releases to a few times a year, violating the agile principle of frequent releases (Agile Alliance, 2001). Fifty percent of survey respondents report that organizational or technical constraints delayed the use of functionalities ready for use. There is, however, a great deal of variation in the duration of delays: 11% of respondents report delays in excess of one year, while the remaining report an average delay of 3.6 weeks.

The project teams in the case study organizations are organized to deal with the integration issue. The primary strategy is to have human resources available to the team that are experts in the integration with the other systems. This reduces the impact of testing and integration with other systems somewhat, but despite these measures the delays in delivery remain significant. In several of the interviews, the impact of the organization's technology was brought up as an explanation for the impossibility of removing this barrier to frequent releases. Two of the case study organizations are changing their database structures to make the systems less interdependent and to allow more frequent releases. However, this is a very expensive and long-term goal.

4.3 The Project Front End

4.3.1 Sprint Zero

The expression *sprint zero* is often used to identify the early activities of an agile project before coding begins. During the interviews, several respondents use the term, but the activities to which they refer vary considerably from one person to another even in the same organization. Of the survey respondents, 73% reported using the term. Table 19 presents the list of the activities that interviewees included in the expression *sprint zero,* followed by the percentage of survey respondents that include these activities in sprint zero. This pattern is very similar to that observed in the case studies.

All of these activities would need to be done early in the project, but most respondents explicitly exclude some of them from what they consider to be the sprint zero. There is obviously a problem of semantics, as the respondents who use the expression *sprint zero* do not agree on its meaning.

4.3.2 System Architecture and Front-End Planning

"The best architectures, requirements, and designs emerge from self-organizing teams" is one of the agile principles (Agile Alliance, 2001). All of the case study projects and all of the survey respondents except three devote time to these activities prior to the beginning of development. One of the exceptions is a team of people doing projects to implement decisions following

Table 19:   Activities Included in Sprint Zero

The planning of sprints	71%
The production of a summary high-level architecture	66%
The writing of user stories for the first sprints	66%
The creation of the product backlog	60%
The creation of epics	51%

the approval of the annual budget in a public organization. The need is considered urgent and the team does this type of project at least annually. In all three exceptions, the project durations and the number of development teams are much less than the average. Survey respondents who do devote time to front-end activities report that on average the time developed to these activities is 54% of what it would have been using traditional methods. However, there is considerable variation: The majority report between 30% and 67%, while 18% report much less (between 1% and 25%), and 21% report that the time devoted is the same as with traditional methods. One respondent reports that more time is devoted to front-end activities with agile approaches. The fact that some survey respondents report no difference is intriguing and deserves further investigation.

Interviewees were asked what proportion of the sprints is planned before development began and the responses vary a great deal. In one case study organization, all of the sprints were planned in detail up front. It should be noted that this case study organization had a strong culture, demanding that projects be well defined prior to approval. In other organizations, only a very small number of sprints was planned in advance. The survey respondents report that on average 35% of sprints are planned up front, but show the same variability, with responses from 0% to 100%. This may be an indication that in some contexts the management of projects has much in common with traditional methods that plan the entire project in detail before starting execution in a plan-driven approach. The survey respondents report that on average 57% of the features actually delivered were in the product backlog at the outset. There is again considerable variation among the responses.

The scope is defined in detail in user stories. These are typically not produced a long time in advance. All the case study organizations and 79% of survey respondents report that user stories are prepared three sprints in advance or less. The most common pattern is, therefore, to produce a summary architecture, to plan one third of sprints, to define more than half of the product backlog prior to beginning development, and to produce user stories one to three sprints in advance during project execution. There is, however, a great deal of variation.

4.4 Project Organizations

All of the projects in the case studies and from the survey have rather large project structures. In addition to the development teams, the project organizations have many other individual members and other committees or teams. The projects from the survey are larger on average than those in the case study organizations and have an average of 94 persons working on the project during the most intensive period, but again with considerable variation. A small proportion of the committees, such as the steering committees and client acceptance committees, have the role of coordinating with the rest of the organization. But the majority of the teams, committees, and individual members play roles in the coordination of the work of the development teams. Specialized personnel on the development teams tend to also be members of the corresponding specialist teams, where the coordination within their area of specialization takes place. Although there is great variety in the particular structures set up to manage each project, there is a common pattern of having a large number of teams or committees and individuals in specialist roles, in addition to the development teams. Roles are shared between members of development teams and teams and/or individuals within the project organization alongside the development teams. For this reason, in order to understand the roles and responsibilities within the project organization, it is necessary to understand the composition and functioning of the development teams and the roles of other teams, committees, and individual specialists. Table 20 presents the percentage of development teams from the survey, with at least one part-time person in each role. Table 21 presents the percentage of projects with each type of specialist team or committee. Table 22 presents both the percentage of projects with at least one part-time specialist and the average number of individual specialists on projects that have at least one part-time person in each role.

Table 20:   Development Team Composition

ScrumMaster	98%
Product owner (PO)	93%
Tester	78%
Tech lead	67%
Business analyst	59%
Developer	57%
Programmer	50%
Programmer/analyst	46%
Architect	46%
Quality assurance	43%
Functional analyst	33%
Documentarist	30%
Agile coach	28%

In addition to the types of teams and committees presented in the table, survey respondents indicate that some project organizations also have strategy committees, core teams, quality assurance teams, teams of tech leads, and program support teams.

Table 21:   Specialist Teams in Project Organizations

Scrum of Scrums	74%
Steering committee	61%
Architecture team	48%
Team of functional testers	46%
Integration team	43%
Team of POs	41%
Client acceptance team	33%
Client decisional committee	17%
Documentation team	7%

Table 22: Individual Specialists in Project Organizations

	Teams with at Least One Part-Time	Average Number Per Team
Project manager	89%	2.3
Program manager	39%	1.1
Architect	37%	1.6
Sponsor	37%	2.0
Product manager	30%	1.6
Product owner	24%	2.2
Agile coach	20%	1.6
Integration tester	15%	2.1
System integrator	15%	2.4
Business analyst	13%	2.5
Tech lead	13%	3.2
Functional tester	11%	3.0
Functional analyst	7%	4.7

In addition to the types of individuals presented in the table, survey respondents indicate that some project organizations also include people in the following roles: quality assurance, change management, line and matrix managers, systems managers, contract managers, operations, security, and executives from end-user organizations.

4.4.1 Development Teams

The recommended size of development teams is seven plus/minus two people (Dingsøyr et al., 2014; Schwaber, 2004; Schwaber & Sutherland, 2013). However, one of the case study projects and 16% of the projects described in the survey have bigger development teams—an average of 12.8 members in the survey results, with 15% of teams having 18 members or more.

The teams in five of the six case study organizations are located geographically within one kilometer of each other and in almost all cases in the same building. The development teams described in the survey are much more geographically dispersed—60% have members in different time zones, which is consistent with the VersionOne (2016) survey results. The differences in geographic dispersion can largely be explained by the differences in the data collection methods, between interviews in organizations in the authors' home city and an online survey.

In all of the case study organizations, Scrum methodology is used. This is consistent with the dominant position of this methodology in the agile community worldwide (VersionOne, 2016). In this methodology, the team members work full-time in close collaboration in open working environments and a hold stand-up meeting at the beginning of each day. All of the case study development teams and 96% of the teams described in the survey have daily stand-up meetings. In all of the case study organizations, working together in open environments is a radical transition from the silos of traditional development. However, only 65% of the development teams in the survey have colocated members and only 57% in open environments.

The composition of development teams indicates that they are multidisciplinary. However, the teams in the case studies are smaller and have fewer specialists in testing, quality assurance, and documentation. These roles are filled in part by other team members and in part by specialists in the project organization outside the development teams. All of the case study projects have a full-time ScrumMaster on each team, and 98% of the development teams described in the survey also have ScrumMasters, some of whom are part-time.

The implementation of agile in traditional software development organizations introduces significant changes in the division of labor and the corresponding role definitions. In traditional development, there are specialized roles that operate largely in silos under a command and control management style. The architects do the high-level design, the functional analysts produce the functional design, the programmers write the code, and the testers qualify the code, which is then integrated into the overall system. At the end of this waterfall-like process, the code is ready to be put into production. At each step, the project is thrown over the wall to the next group. With agile, this is replaced by self-organizing teams with the human resources needed to produce and deliver features that are ready to be demonstrated to customers and introduced into production.

All the case study teams are self-organizing. However, the survey respondents report that this is not the case almost half the time in their projects; on a 7-point Likert scale with the midpoint 4 labeled "As with traditional methods," the average score is 4.15, with values ranging from 1 to 7. There are several possible explanations for this somewhat surprising result. It may be that the specialist teams in traditional development are largely self-organizing and the transition to Scrum is not a radical change in this respect. It may be more difficult to self-organize on larger teams. Self-organizing is much more difficult when team members are not colocated in open environments.

The Scrum methodology places a great deal of emphasis on having stable, full-time membership in teams, and teams learning to work together effectively, thus increasing their velocity or productivity while improving the working climate and employee commitment and satisfaction. In the case study organizations, it takes several months for a new team of people who are not all familiar with agile methods to become effective. All of the case study organizations and 90% of the survey respondents report that there is an effort to maintain stable team composition. The idea of stable teams with full-time membership is in sharp contrast to the functioning of many matrix organizations, in which people are allocated to several projects at one time and more regularly moved between projects.

In the Scrum methodology, development team members are able to do several of the specialized tasks of traditional development. The capacity of people to fill multiple roles and the capacity of people to work on teams are among the criteria used to select projects to be done using agile, as shown in Table 18. In traditional development, the analyst and programmer roles are often distinct, with people in each of these roles unable to do others' tasks. In one of the case study organizations, they are in

separate labor unions, analysts having the status of profession-
als, and programmers that of technicians. This division of labor
causes inefficiencies and hinders the development of mutual
support within the teams. In the case study organizations, the
people volunteering to work on pilot projects were open to the
practice of breaking down this division of labor in the spirit of
helping the team become more productive, but this required the
learning of new skill sets, which takes time. Where agile is well
established, the roles of analyst and of programmer have been
replaced by *programmer/analyst*, a term that has been replaced
in many contexts with *developer*. Table 20 presents the composition of the development teams described in the survey (i.e., the
percentage of teams that include each role, at least part-time).

Because the division of labor among types of developers varies
from one organization to the next, the role descriptors *developer,
programmer, programmer/analyst,* and *functional analyst* are used
in Table 20. The division of labor between analysts and programmers is maintained in the 27% of the survey responses that have
neither developers nor programmer/analysts on development
teams. In some cases, the developers and programmer/analysts are
also involved in testing, particularly where test-driven development
is used, which is the case in 67% of the survey projects.

4.4.2 New and Modified Organizational Roles

The implementation of agile approaches introduces many significant changes in the roles and responsibilities within the organization. It also introduces two new roles—product owner and
ScrumMaster. The need to learn new roles was a central theme of
many of the case study interviews. And as noted in Section 4.2.3,
role definitions not aligned with agile are one of the obstacles to
implementation. Changes to role definitions are one of the most
important impacts of implementing agile in traditional organizations. Survey respondents identify organizational roles that
are modified by the implementation of agile approaches. The response rates are presented in Table 23. The following two sections
examine the new roles of product owner and ScrumMaster. The
modified roles are examined in the following sections.

Table 23: Roles Modified by Implementation of Agile

Project managers	71%
Testers	54%
Business analysts	50%
Developers	50%
Managers	36%
Architects	36%
Functional analysts	32%
Quality assurance officers	29%
Steering committees	21%
Sponsors	21%
Documentarists	21%
Committees that approve projects	14%
Integrators	11%

4.4.3 The Role of Product Owners

The project owner as a new organizational role is central to agile. The typical product owner, as presented in the agile literature (Schwaber, 2004, 2007), is a person who has both the knowledge and the authority to make changes to the product backlog and reprioritize at the beginning of each sprint. In this capacity, the product owner is available to development teams, often on a full-time basis. This role is very different from roles that exist in traditional software development, and it represents a radical departure from previous practice. In the reality of large-scale agile projects, the product owner does not always have the knowledge, authority, and availability as portrayed in this description. The product owner role is often problematic.

The product owner represents the customer, or the end-user organization. A key part of this role is the identification and prioritization of the features in the product backlog at the end of each sprint. In traditional development, there is no mechanism or incentive to make frequent and precise adjustments to priorities, but with agile, this takes place at the beginning of each sprint. The product owner role is radically different from the role of the customer organization in traditional development methods, in which the customer specifies requirements and approves the scope at the outset, approves the project at milestones, makes change requests, and accepts the final product at project closure and commissioning. In traditional development, meetings between customer representatives and project representatives are infrequent and structured in formal approval and change management processes. The customer representative does not meet the members of the development team. In agile, the product owners are members of the project team who meet the ScrumMasters and development teams very frequently, as a minimum at the end of each sprint.

In many cases, the product owners are full-time members of development teams. In two of the case study organizations, there is a product owner on each development team that was responsible for answering team member questions and for preparing the user stories for the upcoming sprints. Most survey respondents (98%) report having product owners on development teams, but in 32% of cases they were part-time. In two case studies and in 60% of the survey responses, hierarchical relationships exist between the product owner on the development team and a product manager or a "chief product owner." The latter is the person to whom the product owners on each development team turn for direction and advice. The product owner teams meet regularly to address issues and establish priorities.

In the other four case studies, there is not a product owner on each team. In three cases, this works very effectively. In two cases, the product owner is a product manager with the authority and responsibility to make decisions regarding priorities for development. Interestingly, the implementation of agile, and particularly, the reprioritization at the beginning of each sprint, and the closer contact between the product owner and the development teams created a context in which these product managers provided more precise and more frequent decisions regarding priorities. In the other case that was effective without having a product owner on each team, there was a very high level of commitment from the customer organization and very good collaboration between the customer organization and the project organization—to the point that they referred to themselves as a team. In the case where the implementation of agile was unsuccessful, the product owner often had insufficient knowledge, availability, and decision-making authority.

The product owner needs to be available, knowledgeable of business needs, and have authority to make decisions. All three of these characteristics pose problems. Making people with these characteristics available to development teams means making them less available for other roles within the business unit, which creates tension around the issue of their availability. In one of the case study organizations, the business units appoint people with very limited availability, business knowledge, and decision-making authority, which in turn causes delays in decisions and many referrals back to those in authority in the business unit, resulting in additional delays. This is a quite hierarchical organization in which managers tend not to delegate very much. The role of product owner in agile is out of sync with this organization's culture. In this case, the difficulties with the product owner role brought major differences between the agile culture and the host organization's culture to the forefront. The results from the other case studies and from the survey show that the situation is often less problematic than that found in this case.

The most critical challenges faced by those for whom the PO is a new role as identified in the survey are presented in Table 24. Both the case study results and the survey results show that the lack of understanding of this new role is the biggest challenge for product owners. In both the case studies and the survey results, the level of support for implementation is lower for business unit managers than for all other groups, and product owners' and business unit and product managers' knowledge of agile is lower than that of other persons directly involved in

Table 24:   Critical Challenges for POs

Understanding the new role	74%
Lack of decision-making authority	55%
Pressure to produce the user stories of the next sprint	52%
Delays in responses to questions	12%

agile development; see Table 16 and Table 17. Both contribute to the lack of understanding of the PO role within the business unit.

Lack of decision-making authority is identified as a challenge, but the survey also indicates that the situation is not catastrophic; on a 7-point Likert scale from "none" to "complete," the PO's decision-making authority is reported as 5.1 on average, with no responses below 3. When a PO does not have complete decision-making authority, he or she must refer to the business unit or product management hierarchy for decisions. Delays in responses can be a challenge, as seen in Table 24, but the survey results show again that the situation is not often catastrophic; on average POs ask for assistance in this regard on a weekly basis and receive a response within four working days. However, outliers with response times of 10 or 15 working days indicate that in some situations the delays are considerable. In one of the case study organizations, a committee of managers from the business unit was set up to respond to such questions. Client decisional committees are also found in 17% of the projects in the survey.

The production of user stories just prior to development of features is an important mechanism within agile approaches that provides flexibility to adapt to changing priorities and to take advantage of the better quality of information close to actual development. Both the case studies and the survey show that in the vast majority of cases user stories are only produced one or two sprints in advance. The POs who are often responsible for this task are, therefore, under pressure to produce the user stories for upcoming sprints.

Where the client is an internal business unit that will use the system in its internal operations, the product owner must know the business and is normally recruited internally. However, the role is different in situations where the system is sold to organizations or people outside the company. In the two case study organizations where the customer is external to the organization, the product owner role is filled by the product management function. There are challenges in this role, particularly when a well-specified product has been sold under contract or when a high-profile customer makes very specific requests. In two of the case study organizations, the use of agile approaches that require the product owner to update, groom, and reprioritize the product backlog had the effect of making the product manager much more responsive to requests for clear direction than had previously been the case.

In the case of systems sold outside the firm, there are additional problems. The marketing and product management departments have both the contact with and the knowledge of customers and markets. The way these departments function traditionally is not in sync with agile approaches that are very flexible and refine priorities at the end of each sprint and frequently produce potential releases. Changing the marketing and product management functions to be in better sync with the agile development approaches is a major organizational change, the detailed study of which is outside the scope of the present research and to the best of our knowledge has not been researched. One of the case study organizations is examining what this might entail. They refer to it as "agile end-to-end," but it has yet to be implemented. A significant part of the problem is the fact that systems are sold under contract and that these contracts specify the scope and the features of the systems to be developed and delivered. The question of how to use the flexibility of agile to deliver systems specified by contract remains largely unanswered. The answer may lie with different types of contracts, but this would mean restructuring the industrial sector, which is neither simple nor without consequences. The increased use of Software as a Service (SaaS) and cloud computing is creating an environment in which agile end-to-end is more feasible (PC Mag Encyclopedia, 2016).

4.4.4 The Roles of ScrumMasters and Agile Coaches

In all the case study organizations, the Scrum methodology is used. This is consistent with the dominant position of this methodology in the agile community worldwide (VersionOne, 2016). The ScrumMaster has a central role in this method. All of the development teams in the case studies and all but one in the survey responses have ScrumMasters. The introduction of ScrumMasters is not problematic because a clear model for the role is well established (Cohn, 2009; Schwaber, 2004, 2007; Sutherland, Viktorov, Blount, & Pintikov, 2007), resources for training and coaches are readily available, and a labor market of trained ScrumMasters exists. In many organizations, experienced ScrumMasters from small projects are available at the time large projects using agile are undertaken. In the case study organizations, the ScrumMasters were mostly programmer/analysts before becoming ScrumMasters. This is a major change, particularly for those who previously had a technical programmer/analyst role. However, in one of the case study organizations, people in team-lead positions became ScrumMasters, which is not seen as a major transition for them.

One of the most common features of the project organizations is the Scrum of Scrums, in which the ScrumMasters meet regularly with other participants, including the project manager. Four of the six case study organizations have such teams, and 74% of the projects described in the survey do as well. VersionOne (2016) reports that the Scrum of Scrums is the most frequently used scaling method. This is an important mechanism for coordination across the project.

The agile coaches work very closely with the ScrumMasters, who are responsible for planning and coordinating the team's work as well as the team processes. There are agile coaches on all the development teams in the case studies—on 28% of the development teams from the survey, and in 20% of the project organizations alongside the development teams.

4.4.5 The Role of Project Managers

As shown in Table 25, the project manager role is often modified by the implementation of agile approaches, but the reported impacts vary a great deal, as shown in Table 23. Only 7% of the survey respondents report that the implementation of agile has had no effect on the project manager role.

The ScrumMasters and the self-organizing teams of agile have taken over the project managers' responsibilities for detailed planning of activities. The changes to the project managers' role in the coordination of development teams show mixed results. In some cases, the coordination between teams is accomplished largely through the Scrum of Scrums. Note, however, that in a small number of cases, the project managers are doing more to coordinate teams, a variability that merits further investigation. The project manager role is also reported to be more strategic and to involve more effort in stakeholder management.

One of the case study organizations experimented with the removal of the project manager role. They concluded that for small projects with only one development team, the project manager role could be filled by the ScrumMaster, but have elected to maintain the role for projects with several development teams. However, in another of the case study organizations and in 11% of the survey responses, the project manager role has

Table 25: The Impact of Agile Implementation on the Project Manager Role

More stakeholder management	62%
Does less detailed planning	59%
Role is more strategic	34%
Does less to coordinate teams	41%
Does more to coordinate teams	28%
No effect	7%

Table 26:   Project Managers

None	11%
One	47%
Two (IT project manager and client project manager)	30%
Multiple project managers by component	13%

been abolished. The way project manager roles are structured varies a great deal, as shown in the survey results presented in Table 26.

The project manager role has changed but is still in place in 89% of the survey responses and in 11 of the 12 case study projects. In three of the case study projects, and in 30% of the survey responses, a structure often found in traditional in-house system development—with two project managers, one from IT and the other from the client organization—has been maintained. However, 13% of the survey responses describe large projects that have been divided into component parts, each with a project manager. The implementation of agile can have a very significant impact on the role of the project manager. A better understanding of the circumstances under which the project manager role changes, and how it changes, is needed.

4.4.6 The Role of Analysts

The role of functional analyst is rare in descriptions of agile in the literature (Hoda, Noble, & Marshall, 2013; Omar, Syed-Abdullah, & Yasin, 2011). Two of the case study organizations have radically different approaches to the role of system analyst. In one organization, the role has been abolished. Another organization has a system analyst on each development team. The other case study organizations have system analysts in the project organization, but not on the development teams. The survey responses indicate that 33% of development teams have functional analysts as development team members, and 7% have individual functional analysts as members of the project organization alongside the development teams. In cases where the ScrumMaster was previously a system analyst, he or she is able to bring this expertise to bear on the project. The question of the role of functional analyst remains largely unresolved.

4.4.7 The Role of Architects

All of the case study organizations have architects in the project organization, but not on the development teams. In most cases, an architecture team is part of the project organization. The survey respondents indicate that 46% of their development teams have architects as members, at least part-time, that 48% of their project organizations have architecture teams, and that 37% of projects have architects as individual members of their project organization. The projects that have both an architecture team and architects on their development teams tend to have architects on the teams on a part-time basis. Architects on the development teams are also members of the architecture teams where these exist. In the case study organizations, functional analysts on development teams are also members of a team led by a system architect. The question of the role of architects and of system analysts brings up the question of how the system architecture is developed on large agile projects. This is the subject of Section 4.3.2 on system architecture and front-end planning. It is clear that most agile project organizations have the specialized human resources necessary for the development of system architecture.

4.5 The Tools and Techniques Employed

Table 27 presents the frequency of use of various tools and techniques associated with agile.

Almost all of the tools and techniques in this list are associated with and used frequently in Scrum development teams. The three most frequently used techniques are central to the Scrum methodology. This result is consistent with those of the Version-One survey (VersionOne, 2016).

Table 27:   Tools and Techniques

Daily stand-up meetings	96%
Product backlog	94%
Retrospectives	92%
Release planning	85%
Estimation of effort by teams	79%
Burndown chart	71%
Backlog grooming	70%
Calculation of velocity	63%
Automatic builds	60%
"Definitions of done" for each sprint	58%
"Definitions of done" for each user story	56%
Open-space environments	54%
Kanban	40%
Online whiteboards	35%

4.6 Scaling Frameworks

The use of scaling frameworks is a more recent phenomenon in the family of agile approaches. It is not the primary focus of investigation in this research. However, information on their use is available from both case study interviews and the survey. Of the six case study organizations, only one declared the use of a scaling framework, which was an in-house mix of Nexus and LeSS. Another case study organization that did not specifically declare that a scaling framework is in use has some of the characteristics of scaling frameworks, including the central concept of release trains and the use of scoping in, rather than the traditional scoping out (Petit & Hobbs, 2010). These terms refer to the practice of defining the total budget and the delivery date of a software version release, but only part of the scope of the release. The balance of the scope is defined as development progresses and priorities develop and become clearer. This organization implemented

Table 28:   Scaling Frameworks

SAFe	5
DAD	2
Nexus	1
LeSS	1

these practices more than five years ago, before the expression *scaling framework* became popular.

Only nine of the survey respondents report using a commercially available scaling framework. The frequencies of use are shown in Table 28. The dominant position of SAFe is consistent with other results (VersionOne, 2016).

4.7 Testing, Integration, and DevOps

DevOps is a more recent trend in agile software development (Gruver & Mouser, 2015; Puppet Labs, 2015; Version One, 2016). It is not a specific subject of investigation in this research. However, it should be noted that DevOps was mentioned during interviews in only two of the case study organizations and no specific questions are included in the survey. However, automated testing, integration, and builds are integral parts of DevOps. Automatic builds are among the tools presented in Table 27, which shows that 60% of respondents report using this tool. However, automated testing, integration, deployment, and monitoring of the performance of systems in production are software engineering practices that can be in place independent of the use of agile in general and DevOps in particular.

It takes several years to implement DevOps, and few organizations have done so successfully to date because both the development of automated tools and the cultural change toward better collaboration among groups of IT specialists take considerable time and effort (Disciplined DevOps, 2016; Gruver & Mouser, 2015; Puppet Labs, 2015). The infrequent mention of DevOps in interviews reflects the current low level of implementation of

DevOps. Further research is needed on this topic, which is likely to become more important as time progresses.

Collaboration between development and operation is central to DevOps, as reflected by the origin of the name. The automatic monitoring and maintenance of systems in production is also central to DevOps. These topics are not mentioned specifically in the case study interviews. Development is conceptualized as a process that delivers software into production with no mention of postproduction activity. In this, the agile implementations are similar to traditional software development practices. In one interview, this is referred to as "water-Scrum-fall." The contact with operations in the agile implementations is through the role of product owner and through demos to operational personnel.

On two update projects in one of the case study organizations, the relations with those responsible for maintenance of the existing system is taken into account. These two projects have been performing very poorly, and system maintenance has been difficult. The cooperation and coordination with operations and maintenance is assured by having people who have worked on system maintenance and/or who worked on the development of the original system on the project teams.

The production of usable software during each sprint is a central concept in agile development, which requires that the software be tested and integrated across development teams and with the overall system. The survey respondents report that the different system components are integrated during every sprint, in 89% of their projects. But how is this accomplished? A significant portion of the testing is done directly on the development teams using test-driven development; 33% of survey respondents report using this tool. It is reasonable to think that they must be using tools that exist in their organization's software engineering environment. The 60% use of automatic builds is indicative of this. Testing and integrating software with several legacy systems, as in all the case study organizations and the majority of the survey responses, is a significant challenge. Two very different approaches are being used to address this issue. The Scrum methodology with the requirement to present demos to user representatives at the end of each sprint and the agile technique of defining and measuring when development of a piece of software is complete or "done" both contribute to producing software that is ready for use and to finding and fixing defects very early in the process. The other approach is to introduce delays for testing and integration prior to release into production, as with traditional methods. The goals of DevOps include providing long-term solutions to these problems.

4.8 The Portrait Provided by the Results

The results from the case studies and from the survey are very consistent. In most cases, the results are very similar, while in a few cases the survey adds detail and perspective to the more limited number of projects and organizations in the case studies. The results are somewhat paradoxical in that some features are common to almost all observations, while others show extreme variability. The common elements are the following:

- Scrum is the dominant methodology and almost all projects have ScrumMasters and do daily stand-up meetings. Agile coaches are used to support Scrum-Masters and development teams.
- Implementation strategies almost always start with pilot projects, which are almost always small and simple projects.
- The activities of the front end include the planning of sprints, the production of a summary architecture, the writing of epics and user stories, and the creation of the product backlog. The time and effort devoted to these activities is significantly less than with traditional methods, but remains important, violating the principle of emergent architecture.
- Approximately two thirds of the scope is defined at the outset in the product backlog, but the detail is provided only one or two sprints in advance in the user stories.

- The project organizations are quite large. In addition to the development teams, the project organizations have several other teams and committees and individuals with specialized expertise, which are responsible for the coordination of the work of the development teams and the technical excellence of their respective areas of specialization.

Within this common pattern, there is considerable variability. Some of the most significant areas of variation are as follows:

- Despite a few common features, the implementation strategies vary significantly.
- The meaning of the term most commonly used to identify the front-end sprint zero varies a great deal even within organizations.
- The extent of front-end planning of sprints varies from almost no planning to the planning of all the sprints prior to approval and initiation.
- All the project organizations are quite big, but there is extreme variability in the detail of these structures.
- The roles of several project participants show significant variability, notably, the roles of project managers, the level of specialization of people involved in development and testing and integration, and the availability and authority of product owners.
- Examples of variability also include the levels of knowledge of agile, support for implementation, resources for change management, extent to which agile approaches are well established or just beginning to be introduced, proportion of projects done using agile, and the delays in releases into production.

Both common patterns and the objects of great variability are important results. From a research perspective, they both identify opportunities for further research.

CHAPTER 5

Discussion

The research questions are:

- At the project level: What challenges are encountered when applying agile to large multiteam software projects and what practices have been developed to alleviate these challenges?
- At the organizational level: How does the context of large, complex organizations affect the adaptation and adoption of agile approaches and vice versa?

5.1 Team Level

Three levels of analysis can be distinguished in the results: the development team, the project, and the organization. The internal functioning of agile development teams is very similar regardless of the number of development teams in the project. Agile approaches are based on self-organized teams in which there is limited specialization among the team members. In a few cases, there was tension between the high level of specialization in the large bureaucratic organizations and the flexibility of agile teams, but this is managed locally within the teams and not a major challenge. Agile team functioning is addressed abundantly in the literature and is not addressed further here.

More differences between small and large projects exist at the project level. Projects with only one development team typically have a limited number of other human resources in the project organization outside the development team. These typically are a product owner and technical specialists, such as architects, analysts, testers, and documentarists. Single development team projects often do not have a project manager, as this role is filled by the ScrumMaster. Larger projects are faced with three organizational challenges: the coordination of multiple development teams, the organization of a greater number of specialists outside the development teams, and the integration with other systems. The three are interrelated.

5.2 Project Level

Larger projects have multiple teams or committees of specialists, including the meeting of ScrumMasters in Scrums of Scrums. When there are product owners on development teams, they meet on a product owner team usually with a more senior product owner or product manager. When specialists are full-time or part-time members of development teams, they typically meet on specialist teams where they deal both with issues related to their area of specialization and with the coordination of the development teams as it related to their specialization. The administrative coordination takes place on the Scrums of Scrums, usually attended by the project manager. Frequent demos, testing, integration, and retrospectives are at the heart of agile. They provide additional opportunities for the coordination among development teams and across areas of specialization.

Large projects also create challenges for the project manager role. Most agree that the impact is significant, but it is difficult to see a generalizable pattern in the adjustments that are taking place. In some situations, project managers are devoting more effort to the coordination of development teams, but in others, less. In a minority of cases, the project manager role has been abolished. Most agree, however, that where the project manager role has been maintained, it has become more strategic and focused more on stakeholder management. It is too early in the evolution of the management of large agile projects to come to a definite conclusion on this subject.

5.3 Interaction Between the Project and the Organization

Most other challenges are related to the interaction between the projects and the organization. The implementation of agile in a large organization with well-established traditional methods is a significant organizational change. As with any significant change, management support is critical (Young & Poon, 2013). The acceptance and support of IT and business unit managers, as well as development personnel, are also very important. Being knowledgeable of agile is a necessary condition for support.

One of the biggest challenges is the relationship between the project and the client organization, which is related to the challenges with the role of product owner. The transition from traditional methods to agile approaches is a radical change. In addition, business unit managers are on average less knowledgeable and less supportive of agile. Collaboration between the project and the business unit managers is critical. Note that it was the primary explanation for the outstanding success of one of the case study projects.

Agile approaches require business unit managers and product managers to be more involved in projects, to commit significant resources, to better prioritize their needs, and to respond more quickly to requests for clarification of business rules and priorities. They also create ambiguity as to the exact nature and scope of the project deliverable. Two elements are key to the creation of an effective working relationship between the business unit and the project—first, the creation of a partnership between the customer organization and the project based on a clear understanding of each other's context and needs, and second, the role of product owner. One cannot be effective without the other.

5.4 Conflicts Between Large Traditional Organizations and Agile Principles

There are conflicts between large traditional organizations and agile principles that are related to structures, processes, and culture (Iivari & Iivari, 2011). One of the biggest challenges is the difference in role definitions between the two. The solution organizations have adopted is to use pilot projects to isolate the problem and to develop the new role definitions. The project approval process in traditional organizations that requires project parameters be well defined in advance is another significant challenge, which is both a process and a cultural issue. For internal projects, the solution has again been negotiating special arrangements on pilot projects. For projects with contracts with external customers, the issue is as yet unresolved, especially in relation to scope definition. A change in leadership style from command and control to styles approaching servant leadership is again a very significant change that organizations are addressing on pilot projects (Greenleaf, 2002). It is too early in the evolution of these changes to know how they will develop in the future.

5.5 A Period of Experimentation

The use of agile on large projects in large organizations is a relatively new phenomenon for which clear guidance is not available. There are conflicts between agile approaches and principles and traditional software development in large bureaucratic organizations. Organizations are experimenting, as shown by the extreme variability of the responses to most of the survey questions. On average, the organizations in both the case studies and the survey have been using agile on large projects for three years. With an average duration of one-and-a-half years, a large number of organizations have completed only a small number of large agile projects. The majority of large organizations are therefore still at a stage of experimental implementation.

There are several current trends within the field of agile software development. Some are more well established than others. The development of agile is both responding to and driving the experimentation in large organizations. The use of Scrum methodology in development teams is well understood and well established. The application of this method to multiple development teams does not pose a serious challenge. However, the means for coordinating multiple development teams and multiple areas of technical expertise have not been well established, nor have the roles of project manager and product owner. The focus of the present research is to examine and document the current experimentation at the level of using agile on projects with multiple development teams.

While organizations continue to experiment at this level, two other important and more recent trends in agile development are starting to have a significant impact of software development methods and the organizational arrangements that accompany them. At a more macro level, scaling frameworks are changing project portfolio management and release planning. At the same time, DevOps is changing software engineering practices. Some organizations are implementing one or the other or both. These changes take several years to implement, in part because DevOps includes both technological changes to automate testing, integration, and deployment as well as cultural changes to improve collaboration among the specialized groups involved in software development. The rate of change in software development induced by the introduction of agile is accelerating. The period of experimentation is likely to continue for several years.

CHAPTER 6

Conclusion

Agile approaches are being used more and more on large software projects in large organizations. The use of agile in this context requires significant adaptations at both the project and the organization levels. There are fundamental contradictions between large bureaucratic organizations with well-established traditional software development methods and agile principles and practices. The resolution of these contradictions is currently ongoing, but as yet incomplete. Some aspects of the form these will take in the future are already quite clear, but others will only become clear as the evolutionary process progresses—a subject that will require further research with continued adoption and adaptation.

CHAPTER 7

Future Research

Some of the most important outstanding questions are the following:

- What will be the project manager's role in the future? Will there be project managers in this type of context? Will the answers to these questions be contingent upon as yet unidentified conditions?
- Projects with internal business units as customers are in a situation quite different from those with external customers under contract.
  - For internal projects, how will the relationship between business units and projects evolve and will this fundamentally change the entire organization?
  - For external projects, how will the use of agile for systems development affect the entire organization with a redefinition of the roles of other departments and the relationship with customers in what might become "agile end-to-end"?

- The results of the present research indicate that organizational and project size affect the implementation and use of agile and that differences between public and private organizations have less of an effect. More research is needed to develop a good understanding of contingency effects.
- To date, the effect of the use of agile has been primarily at the project level, with little or no reconceptualization at the program or portfolio level. However, scaling frameworks that propose solutions at these levels are gaining in popularity. How will agile affect program and portfolio management?
- DevOps is the most recent trend in agile software development. What effects will it have?

Acknowledgments

This research was funded in part by the Project Management Institute's Sponsored Research Program. PMI also assisted in data collection for the survey.

References

Abrahamsson, P., Conboy, K., & Xiaofeng, W. (2009). "Lots done, more to do:" The current state of agile systems development research. [Editorial]. *European Journal of Information Systems, 18*, 281–284.

Abrahamsson, P., Warsta, J., Siponen, M. T., & Ronkainen, J. (2003). *New directions on agile methods: A comparative analysis.* Paper presented at the 25th International Conference on Software Engineering, Portland, OR.

Agile Alliance. (2001). *Manifesto for agile software development.* Retrieved from http://agilemanifesto.org/

Al-Zoabi, Z. (2008). *Introducing discipline to Xp: Applying Prince2 on XP Projects.* Paper presented at the Information and Communication Technologies: From Theory to Applications. ICTTA 2008. 3rd International Conference on Information & Communication Technologies, Damascus, Syria.

Ambler, S. W. (2009). *The agile scaling model (ASM): Adapting agile methods for complex environments.* Somers, NY: IBM Corporation.

Ambler, S. W., & Lines, M. (2014). *Scaling agile software development disciplined agility at scale.* Retrieved from disciplinedagileconsortium.org

Anantatmula, V. S., & Anantatmula, M. (2008). *Use of agile methodology for IT consulting projects.* Paper presented at the PMI Research Conference, Warsaw, Poland.

Balaji, S., & Murugaiyan, S. (2012). Waterfall vs. V-Model vs. agile: A comparative study on SDLC. *International Journal of Information Technology and Business Management, 2*(1), 26–29.

Barlow, J. B., Keith, M. J., Wilson, D. W., Schuetzler, R. M., Lowry, P. B., Vance, A., & Giboney, J. S. (2011). Overview and guidance on agile development in large organizations. *Communications of the Association for Information Systems, 29*, 25–44.

Boehm, B. (2002). Get ready for agile methods, with care. *Computer, 35*(1), 64–69.

Boehm, B., & Turner, R. (2003). *Observations on balancing discipline and agility*. Paper presented at the Agile Development Conference, Salt Lake City, UT.

Boehm, B., & Turner, R. (2004). *Balancing agility and discipline: A guide for the perplexed*. Boston, MA: Addison-Wesley.

Boehm, B., & Turner, R. (2005). Management challenges to implementing agile processes in traditional development organizations. *IEEE Software, 22*(5), 30–39.

Carstens, D. S., Richardson, G. L., & Smith, R. B. (2013). *Project management tools and techniques: A practical guide*. Boca Raton, FL: CRC Press.

Cohn, M. (2009). *Succeeding with agile: Software development using Scrum*. Upper Saddle River, NJ: Pearson Education.

Conboy, K. (2009). Agility from first principles: Reconstructing the concept of agility in information systems development. *Information Systems Research, 20*(3), 329–354.

Conforto, E. C., Amaral, D. C., da Silva, S. L., Di Felippo, A., & Kamikawachi, D. S. L. (2016). The agility construct on project management theory. *International Journal of Project Management, 34*(4), 660–674.

Conforto, E. C., Rebentisch, E., & Amaral, D. C. (2014). *Project management agility global survey*. Cambridge, MA: MIT Consortium for Engineering Program Excellence.

Conforto, E. C., Salum, F., Amaral, D. C., da Silva, S. L., & de Almeida, L. F. M. (2014). Can agile project management be adopted by industries other than software development? *Project Management Journal, 45*(3), 21–34.

Dikert, K., Paasivaara, M., & Lassenius, C. (2016). Challenges and success factors for large-scale agile transformations: A systematic literature review. *Journal of Systems & Software, 119*, 87–108.

Dingsøyr, T., Fægri, T. E., & Itkonen, J. (2014). What is large in large-scale? A taxonomy of scale for agile software development product-focused software process improvement (Vol. 8892 of the series *Lecture Notes in Computer Science*), pp. 273–276). Berlin, Germany: Springer.

Dingsøyr, T., & Moe, N. B. (2013). *Research challenges in large-scale agile software development.* Paper presented at the ACM SIG-SOFT, *Software Engineering Notes.* Paper presented at XP2013 conference in Vienna, Austria, in June 2013. Proceedings in the ACM SIGSOFT, *Software Engineering Notes.*

Dingsøyr, T., & Moe, N. B. (2014). Towards principles of large-scale agile development: A summary of the workshop at XP2014 and a revised research agenda agile methods. *Large-Scale Development, Refactoring, Testing, and Estimation* (Volume 199 of the series *Lecture Notes in Business Information Processing,* pp. 1–8). Berlin, Germany: Springer.

Dingsøyr, T., Nerur, S., Balijepally, V., & Moe, N. B. (2012). A decade of agile methodologies: Towards explaining agile software development. *Journal of Systems and Software, 85*(6), 1213–1221.

Disciplined Agile Delivery (DAD). (2015). Retrieved from http://www.disciplinedagiledelivery.com/

Disciplined DevOps. (2016). Disciplined agile 2.0—A process decision framework for enterprise I.T. Retrieved from http://www.disciplinedagiledelivery.com/disciplineddevops/

Dyba, T., & Dingsøyr, T. (2008). Empirical studies of agile software development: A systematic review. *Information and Software Technology, 50,* 833–859.

Elshamy, A., & Elssamadisy, A. (2007). Applying agile to large projects: New agile software development practices for large projects. In G. Concas, E. Damiani, M. Scotto & G. Succi (Eds.), *Agile processes in software engineering and extreme programming* (Vol. 4536, pp. 46–53). Berlin, Heidelberg, Germany: Springer.

Fernandez, D. J., & Fernandez, J. D. (2008). Agile project management—Agilism versus traditional approaches. *Journal of Computer Information Systems, 49*(2), 10–17.

Fitzgerald, B., Stol, K.-J., O'Sullivan, R., & O'Brien, D. (2013). *Scaling agile methods to regulated environments: An industry case study.* Paper presented at the Proceedings of the 2013 International Conference on Software Engineering, San Francisco, CA.

Freudenberg, S., & Sharp, H. (2010). The top 10 burning research questions from practitioners. *Software, IEEE, 27*(5), 8–9.

Gartner. (2016). *Bimodal*. Retrieved from from http://www.gartner .com/it-glossary/bimodal/

Gat, I. (2006). *How BMC is scaling agile development*. Paper presented at the IEEE Agile 2006 Conference, Minneapolis, MN.

Goh, J. C.-L., Pan, S. L., & Zuo, M. (2013). Developing the agile is development practices in large-scale IT projects: The trust-mediated organizational controls and IT project team capabilities perspectives. *Journal of the Association for Information Systems, 14*(12), 722–756.

Greenleaf, R. K. (2002). *Servant leadership: A journey into the nature of legitimate power and greatness* (25th anniversary ed.). Costa Mesa,CA: Paulist Press.

Grewal, H., & Maurer, F. (17–20 August 2007). *Scaling agile methodologies for developing a production accounting system for the oil & gas industry*. Paper presented at the Agile Conference (AGILE 2007), Washington, DC.

Gruver, G., & Mouser, T. (2015). *Leading the transformation: Applying agile and devops principles at scale*. Portland, OR: IT Revolution.

Gruver, G., Young, M., & Fulghum, P. (2013). *A practical approach to large-scale agile developement—How HP transformed LaserJet Futuresmart firmware*. Upper Saddle River, NJ: Addison-Wesley.

Highsmith, J. A. (2003). Cutter consortium reports: Agile project management: principles and tools. *Cutter Consortium, 4*(2), 2–4.

Highsmith, J. A. (2010). *Agile project management—Creating innovative products*. Upper Saddle River, NJ: Addison-Wesley.

Hobbs, A., & Petit, Y. (2017). Agile methods on large projects in large organizations. *Project Management Journal, 48*(3), 3–19.

Hoda, R., Noble, J., & Marshall, S. (2013). Self-organizing roles on agile software development teams. *IEEE Transactions on Software Engineering, 39*(3), 422–444.

Iivari, J., & Iivari, N. (2011). The relationship between organizational culture and the deployment of agile methods. *Information and Software Technology, 53*(5), 509–520.

Karlström, D., & Runeson, P. (2005). Combining agile methods with stage-gate project management. *IEEE Software, 22*(3), 43–49.

Karlström, D., & Runeson, P. (2006). Integrating agile software development into stage-gate managed product development. *Empirical Software Engineering, 11*(2), 203–225.

Kettunen, P. (2007). Extending software project agility with new product development enterprise agility. *Software Process: Improvement and Practice, 12*(6), 541–548.

Kettunen, P. (2009a). Adopting key lessons from agile manufacturing to agile software product development—A comparative study. *Technovation, 29*(6/7), 408.

Kettunen, P. (2009b). *Agile software development in large-scale new product development organization: Team-level perspective.* Doctoral dissertation, Helsinki University of Technology (TKK Dissertations 186).

Kettunen, P., & Laanti, M. (2008). Combining agile software projects and large-scale organizational agility. *Software Process: Improvement and Practice, 13*(2), 183—193.

Kniberg, H., & Ivarsson, A. (2012). *Scaling agile @ Spotify.* Retrieved from http://blog.beule.fr/contenus/2013/02/Spotify-Scaling.pdf

Kruchten, P. (2013). Contextualizing agile software development. *Journal of Software: Evolution and Process, 25*(4), 351–361.

Laanti, M. (2012). *Agile methods in large-scale software development organizations applicability and model for adoption.* Doctoral dissertation, University of Oulu—Faculty of Science, Department of Information Processing Science.

Laanti, M., Salo, O., & Abrahamsson, P. (2011). Agile methods rapidly replacing traditional methods at Nokia: A survey of opinions on agile transformation. *Information and Software Technology, 53*(3), 276–290.

Laanti, M., Similä, J., Abrahamsson, P., & Delta, N. (2013). Definitions of agile software development and agility. In *Systems, Software and Services Process Improvement* (pp. 247–258). Berlin, Heidelberg, Germany: Springer.

Larman, C. (2004). *Agile and iterative development: A manager's guide.* Upper Saddle River, NJ: Addison-Wesley.

Larman, C. (2015). *LeSS.* Retrieved from http://less.works/

Larman, C., & Vodde, B. (2013). Scaling agile development—Large and multisite product development with large-scale scrum. *CrossTalk* (May–June), 8–12.

Larman, C., & Vodde, B. (2014). *Large-scale Scrum: More with LeSS.* Upper Saddle River, NJ: Addison Wesley Professional.

Leffingwell, D. (2010). *Agile software requirements: Lean requirements practices for teams, programs, and the enterprise.* Upper Saddle River, NJ: Addison-Wesley.

Leffingwell, D. (2015). *Safe—Scaled agile framework.* Retrieved from http://www.scaledagileframework.com/

Levin, G. (2012). *Program management: A life cycle approach.* Boca Raton, FL: CRC Press, Auerbach Publications.

Lindvall, M., Muthig, D., Dagnino, A., Wallin, C., Stupperich, M., Kiefer, D., & Kahkonen, T. (2004). Agile software development in large organizations. *Computer, 37*(12), 26–34.

Mahanti, A. (2006). Challenges in enterprise adoption of agile methods—A survey. *Journal of Computing and Information Technology, 3,* 197–206.

McAvoy, J., & Butler, T. (2009). A failure to learn by software developers: Inhibiting the adoption of an agile software development methodology. *Journal of Information Technology Case and Application Research, 11*(1), 23–46.

Mintzberg, H. (1979). *The structuring of organizations—A synthesis of the research.* Englewood Cliffs, NJ: Prentice-Hall.

Misra, S. C., Kumar, V., & Kumar, U. (2009). Identifying some important success factors in adopting agile software development practices. *Journal of Systems and Software, 82*(11), 1869–1890.

Omar, M., Syed-Abdullah, S.-L., & Yasin, A. (2011). The impact of agile approach on software engineering teams. *American Journal of Economics and Business Administration, 3*(1), 12–17.

Paasivaara, M., Durasiewicz, S., & Lassenius, C. (2008a). *Distributed agile development: Using Scrum in a large project.* Paper presented at the IEEE International Conference on Global Software Engineering, 2008 (ICGSE 2008), Banagalore, India.

Paasivaara, M., Durasiewicz, S., & Lassenius, C. (2008b). Using Scrum in a globally distributed project: A case study. *Software Process: Improvement and Practice, 13*(6), 527544.

Paasivaara, M., & Lassenius, C. (22–23 September 2011). *Scaling Scrum in a large distributed project.* Paper presented at International Symposium on the Empirical Software Engineering and Measurement (ESEM 2011), Banff, Alberta, Canada.

Papadopoulos, G. (2015). Moving from traditional to agile software development methodologies also on large, distributed projects. *Procedia–Social and Behavioral Sciences, 175,* 455–463.

PC Mag Encyclopedia. (2016). *Definition of SaaS*. Retrieved from http://www.pcmag.com/encyclopedia/term/56112/saas

Petit, Y., & Besner, C. (2013). *Project and multi-project agility: Scaling challenges in a large multi-national organization.* Paper presented at the International Research Conference on Organising by Projects (IRNOP), Oslo, Norway.

Petit, Y., & Hobbs, B. (2010). *Project portfolios: Trains not funnels.* Paper presented at the EURAM, Rome, Italy.

Petit, Y., & Lévesque, M.-M. (2015). *Assessing the application of agile principles in non-IT projects.* Paper presented at the IRNOP, London, England.

Project Management Institute. (2012). *A guide to the project management body of knowledge (PMBOK® guide)* – Fifth edition. Newtown Square, PA: Author.

Puppet Labs. (2015). *2015 state of devops report.* Retrieved from https://puppet.com/resources/white-paper/2015-state-of-devops-report

Rautiainen, K., von Schantz, J., & Vahaniitty, J. (2011). *Supporting scaling agile with portfolio management: Case Paf.Com.* Paper presented at the 2011 44th Hawaii International Conference on System Sciences (HICSS), Kauai, HI.

Razavi, A. M., & Ahmad, R. (2014). *Agile development in large and distributed environments—A systematic literature review on organizational, managerial and cultural aspects.* Paper presented at the 8th Malaysian Software Engineering Conference (MySEC), Kuala Lumpur, Malaysia.

Scaled Agile Framework. (2014). Retrieved from from http://scaledagileframework.com/

Schwaber, K. (2004). *Agile project management with Scrum.* Redmond, WA: Microsoft Press.

Schwaber, K. (2007). *The enterprise and Scrum.* Redmond, WA: Microsoft Press.

Schwaber, K. (2015). *Nexus.* Retrieved from https://www.scrum.org/Resources/The-Nexus-Guide

Schwaber, K., & Sutherland, J. (2013). *The Scrum guide™: The definitive guide to Scrum: The rules of the game.* Retrieved from http://www.scrumguides.org/

Sheffield, J., & Lemétayer, J. (2013). Factors associated with the software development agility of successful projects. *International Journal of Project Management, 31*(3), 459–472.

Sheskin, D. J. (2007). *Handbook of parametric and nonparametric statistical procedures* (4th ed.). London, England: Chapman & Hall.

Sommer, A. F., Hedegaard, C., Dukovska-Popovska, I., & Steger-Jensen, K. (2015). Improved product development performance through agile/stage-gate hybrids. *Research Technology Management, 58*(1), 34–44.

Špundak, M. (2014). Mixed agile/traditional project management methodology—Reality or illusion? *Procedia—Social and Behavioral Sciences, 119*(0), 939–948.

Stettina, C. J., & Hörz, J. (2015). Agile portfolio management: An empirical perspective on the practice in use. *International Journal of Project Management, 33*(1), 140–152.

Stojanov, I., Turetken, O., & Trienekens, J. J. M. (2015). *A maturity model for scaling agile development.* Paper presented at the 41st Euromicro Conference on Software Engineering and Advanced Applications (SEAA 2015), Funchal, Madeira, Portugal.

Sutherland, J., Viktorov, A., Blount, J., & Pintikov, N. (2007). *Distributed Scrum: Agile project management with outsourced development teams.* Paper presented at the Hawaii International Conference on System Sciences, Waikaloa, HI.

Tashakkori, A., & Teddlie, C. (1998). *Mixed methodology: Combining qualitative and quantitative approaches* (Vol. 46). Thousand Oaks, CA: Sage.

Thomke, S., & Reinertsen, D. (1998). Agile product development: Managing development flexibility in uncertain environments. *California Management Review, 41*(1), 8–30.

VersionOne. (2016). *10th annual state of agile report.* Retrieved from https://versionone.com/pdf/VersionOne-10th-Annual-State -of-Agile-Report.pdf

Vinekar, V., Slinkman, C. W., & Nerur, S. (2006). Can agile and traditional systems development approaches coexist? An ambidextrous view. *Information Systems Management, 23*(3), 31–42.

Young, R., & Poon, S. (2013). Top management support—Almost always necessary and sometimes sufficient for success: Findings from a fuzzy set analysis. *International Journal of Project Management, 31*(7), 943–957.

Appendix

Context

Research Project:

- **Investigation of the use of agile methods on big projects in big organizations.**
- **Carried out by Yvan Petit and Brian Hobbs, professors at the University of Quebec, Montreal School of Management's Project Management Research Chair.**
- **Supported by the PMI Sponsored Research Program.**
- **Case studies have already been done. Preliminary results were presented at the PMI-Montreal Symposium 7 October 2015.**

The objective of this survey is to validate and enrich the results of the case studies.

This research project has an ethics certificate issued by the university. All of the data collected will therefore remain anonymous and confidential.

Please complete this survey if you:

- **work in an organization with more than 2,000 employees, and**
- **that uses agile methods to execute software projects with three development teams or more.**

Completing the survey should take you about 15 minutes.

Demographic Information:

1. Your age?

   [ ]

2. Your sex?

   ○ Male

   ○ Female

3. How many years of experience do you have with agile methods?

   [ ]

4. Your level of education?

   ○ Junior college or high school

   ○ Undergraduate degree

   ○ Graduate degree

The Organizational Context

5. The organization is:

   ○ Private

   ○ Public

   ○ Nonprofit

In the next section of the survey, you will be asked to describe a large project employing agile methods that has been completed or is close to completion. The relevant organizational context for the understanding of this project may be the entire organization or only a part of the organization.

6. The relevant context is:

    ◯ The entire organization

    ◯ A part of the organization (e.g., a division or a subsidiary)

7. There are approximately how many employees in the entire organization?

    ☐

8. If the relevant context is only part of the organization, what is the approximate number of employees?

    ☐

In the rest of the survey, please respond relative to the relevant organizational context.

9. What is the primary activity of the organization?

    ◯ Information technology

    ◯ Telecommunications

    ◯ Software development

    ◯ Financial services

    ◯ Engineering

    ◯ Construction

    ◯ Manufacturing

    ◯ New product development

    ◯ Training/education

    ◯ Health services

    ◯ Consulting (other than engineering or IT)

    ◯ Other (Please specify)

    ☐

10. In what year were agile methods used for the first time on large or small projects?

    ☐

11. In what year were agile methods used for the first time on large projects (with three development teams or more)?

    ☐

12. What is your organization's level of maturity in the use of agile methods on large or small projects? Scale inspired by CMMI.

    ○ "Initial" – ad hoc; relies on the competency of individuals, not the organization

    ○ "Managed" – there is a method based on previous experience

    ○ "Defined" – common, organization-wide understanding of agile methods, roles, and responsibilities

    ○ "Managed quantitatively" – stable and measured and controlled processes

    ○ "Optimizing" – focus to ensure a continuous improvement process is in place

13. If there was a community of practice on agile, what year was it created?

    ☐

14. Approximately how many projects are under way at the same time in this organization?

    ☐

15. Of these, how many use agile methods?

    ☐

Description of a Specific Project

For the rest of the survey, please respond relative to a specific large project that used agile methods, a project that has been completed or is close to completion.

16. Your primary role in this project:

- ◯ Manager (IT)
- ◯ Manager (business or product unit)
- ◯ Project manager
- ◯ Program manager
- ◯ Portfolio manager
- ◯ Manager (other)
- ◯ ScrumMaster
- ◯ Agile coach
- ◯ Product owner (PO)
- ◯ Business analyst
- ◯ Functional analyst
- ◯ Programmer/analyst
- ◯ Programmer
- ◯ Tester
- ◯ Architect
- ◯ Other (Please specify)

```


```

17. How many sprints were there in this project?

```


```

18. What was the average duration of sprints (in weeks)?

    [   ]

19. The project deliverable is?

    ○ Used primarily by employees of the organization

    ○ Used primarily by customers of the organization

    ○ Used as much by employees as by customers of the organization

    ○ Sold to organizations for use in their internal systems

    ○ Sold to individuals (e.g., software for income taxes, pacemakers, or videogames)

    ○ Other (Please specify)

    [   ]

20. If the majority of users are in one country, please identify the country.

    [   ]

21. If the product is sold to multiple organizations or individuals, who filled the PO role?

    ○ People from product management or marketing

    ○ Other (Please specify)

    [   ]

22. If the product is sold to multiple organizations or individuals, in what country are the people who filled the PO role located?

    [   ]

23. Does the product have a hardware component?

○ Yes

○ No

24. The deliverable was?

○ An update of an existing system or product

○ A new system or product

25. If it was an update, how many versions were maintained at the same time (including the one under development)?

[   ]

26. The structure of the organization close to the project was?

Functional	Weak matrix	Balanced matrix	Strong matrix	By project
1	2	3	4	5
○	○	○	○	○

27. With how many other systems was the deliverable of this project integrated?

[   ]

28. Did organizational or technical constraints delay the use of functionalities ready for use? If yes, indicate the number of weeks of delay. If not, respond 0.

[   ]

29. At the time the project started, what was the level of knowledge of agile methods of people involved in this project?

	Very weak 1	2	3	Average 4	5	6	Very strong 7
Upper management	O	O	O	O	O	O	O
Management of IT	O	O	O	O	O	O	O
Members of the development teams	O	O	O	O	O	O	O
Business unit or product managers	O	O	O	O	O	O	O
POs	O	O	O	O	O	O	O
Project manager	O	O	O	O	O	O	O

The Project Organization

30. How many people worked on the project during the most intensive period (full-time equivalent)?

> [   ]

Please describe the project organization relative to the following three components:

1. Development teams

31. What was the maximum number of development teams?

> [   ]

32. In how many of these teams were the members colocated?

> [   ]

33. Were all the development teams located within one kilometer of each other?

○ Yes

○ No

34. Were all the development teams in the same time zone?

○ Yes

○ No

35. In what country did the majority of the people who worked on this project live?

[   ]

36. On average, how many people were on each development team?

[   ]

37. What was the typical composition of a development team? Please indicate the number of people in full-time equivalents. For those who are part-time on the project, please indicate a proportion (0.25 for 25%). The total should be the same as the answer to the previous question.

ScrumMaster

```

```

Agile coach

```

```

Product owner (PO)

```

```

Business analyst

```

```

Functional analyst

```

```

Tech lead

```

```

Programmer/analyst

```

```

Programmer

```

```

Developer

```

```

Tester

Quality assurance

Architect

Documentarist

Other (Please specify the number of people and their roles)

2. Other teams or committees

38. Committees/teams related to the project

☐ Scrum of Scrum

☐ Team of POs

☐ Team of functional testers

☐ Integration team

☐ Client acceptance team

☐ Documentation team

☐ Architecture team

☐ Client decisional committee

☐ Steering committee

☐ Other (Please specify)

3. Individuals who are members of the project organization

39. Individuals who are members of the project organization but not in the committees or teams referred to in the previous question (full-time equivalents):

Product owner

[   ]

Product manager

[   ]

Business analyst

[   ]

Functional analyst

[   ]

Tech lead

[   ]

Architect

[   ]

System integrator

[   ]

Functional tester

[   ]

Integration tester

[ ]

Project manager

[ ]

Agile coach

[ ]

Program manager

[ ]

Sponsor

[ ]

Other (Please specify the number of people and their roles)

[ ]

40. Was there one or more project managers on this project?

O Yes, only one

O Yes, two: an IT project manager and a client project manager

O No

O Other (Please specify)

[ ]

41. If there was more than one person in the PO role, was there a hierarchy among these people?

O Yes

O No

42. To what extent were development teams self-organized?

Much less than with traditional methods			As with traditional methods			Much more than with traditional methods
1	2	3	4	5	6	7
○	○	○	○	○	○	○

43. Was there an effort to maintain stable team composition?

○ Yes

○ No

44. If employees with other roles have become Scrum-Masters, what was their previous role? (If all Scrum-Masters were specially employed for this role, either as consultants or employees, please do not answer this question.)

☐ Architect

☐ Programmer/analyst

☐ Project manager

☐ Functional analyst

☐ Other (Please specify)

[   ]

45. What were the roles of POs before they filled this role?

☐ Operational personnel in the customer organization

☐ Business analyst

☐ Other (Please specify)

[   ]

46. What was the decision-making power of POs?

None			Average			Complete
1	2	3	4	5	6	7
○	○	○	○	○	○	○

47. In cases where the POs did not have complete decisional autonomy:

At what frequency did they refer to the hierarchy for decisions?

How quickly did they receive a response? (Number of working days)

Architecture and the Beginning of the Project

"Emergent architecture" is one of the agile principles. However, we have observed activities related to architecture and to the planning of sprints before the beginning of software development per se.

48. Do you use the expression *sprint zero*?

○ Yes

○ No

49. It yes, this expression refers to what activities?

☐ Production of a summary high-level architecture

☐ The planning of sprints

☐ The creation of the product backlog

☐ The creation of epics

☐ The writing of user stories for the first sprints

☐ Other (Please specify)

[   ]

50. How many weeks were devoted to the activities in the previous question prior to the commencement of development as such?

[   ]

51. If this project had been done using traditional methods, how many weeks would have been devoted to the activities in question 49 prior to the beginning of development as such?

[   ]

4. Sprint planning

52. For how many development sprints was the planning done prior to the beginning of development?

[   ]

53. Sprints were planned and executed:

○ One after another

○ By groups of sprints as a function of a delivery or a release

54. If by groups of sprints, how many sprints were there in each group?

[_____]

55. During the project, user stories were written for how many sprints in advance?

[_____]

56. Was there a release plan?

○ Yes

○ No

57. How many releases were there during this project?

[_____]

5. The creation of a product backlog

58. Was there a product backlog for the entire project?

○ Yes

○ No

59. What percentage of the features actually produced were included in the product backlog at the time when development started?

[_____]

6. Retrospectives

60. Did retrospectives take place at the end of each sprint?

○ Yes

○ No

61. Which of the following statements best describes the retrospectives in this project?

☐ Each team had a retrospective.

☐ There was a retrospective with the members of all the teams.

☐ There was a retrospective with representatives of all the teams.

☐ Other (Please specify)

```
┌─────────────────────────────────────────────┐
│                                             │
└─────────────────────────────────────────────┘
```

7. Demos and integration

62. What was the frequency of demos of the functionalities produced in each team?

○ During each sprint

○ At the end of each sprint

After how many sprints?

```
┌─────────────────────────────────────────────┐
│                                             │
└─────────────────────────────────────────────┘
```

63. What was the frequency of demos integrating the functionalities produced by all the teams?

   ⭕ At the end of each sprint

   After how many sprints?

   [   ]

64. At what frequency were the different components integrated?

   ⭕ During each sprint

   ⭕ At the end of each sprint

   After how many sprints?

   [   ]

65. If a new priority feature was identified during the project, how many weeks elapsed between the time it was identified and the time it was released?

   [   ]

Tools and Techniques

66. Which techniques were used during this project?
    - ☐ Daily stand-up meetings
    - ☐ Product backlog
    - ☐ Retrospectives
    - ☐ Release planning
    - ☐ Backlog grooming
    - ☐ Burndown chart
    - ☐ Estimation of effort by teams
    - ☐ Calculation of velocity
    - ☐ Definitions of done for each user story
    - ☐ Definitions of done for each sprint
    - ☐ Automatic builds
    - ☐ Open-space environments
    - ☐ Online whiteboards
    - ☐ Kanban
    - ☐ Other (Please specify)

67. Was a scaling framework used on this project?
    - ○ Yes
    - ○ No

68. If yes, which one?

☐ SAFe

☐ NEXUS

☐ LeSS

☐ DAD

☐ Other (Please specify)

```
┌─────────────────────────────────────────────┐
│                                             │
└─────────────────────────────────────────────┘
```

69. Was Test-Driven Development (TDD) used on this project?

◯ Yes

◯ No

70. TDD is used on what percentage of projects in this organization?

```
┌──────────────┐
│              │
└──────────────┘
```

71. Which of the following statements best describes pair programming as practiced in this project?

◯ Pair programming was used systematically.

◯ The code was seen systematically by at least two team members.

◯ Verification of the code by a second party was informal and nonsystematic.

◯ There was no pair programming.

Performance

72. How would you describe the success of this project relative to projects using traditional methods in your organization?

Much less successful			Equivalent			Much more successful
1	2	3	4	5	6	7
O	O	O	O	O	O	O

73. How would you describe the success of this project relative to other projects in your organization using agile methods?

Much less successful			Equivalent			Much more successful
1	2	3	4	5	6	7
O	O	O	O	O	O	O

74. How would you describe the success of this project relative to projects in other organizations in your sector of activity?

Much less successful			Equivalent			Much more successful
1	2	3	4	5	6	7
O	O	O	O	O	O	O

75. What were the benefits of the use of agile methods?

- ☐ More rapid delivery to customers
- ☐ Better adapted to customer needs
- ☐ Development of fewer features that are never used
- ☐ Better collaboration among organizational units
- ☐ More centered on the creation of business value
- ☐ Better prioritization
- ☐ Code of better quality
- ☐ Documentation that is better adapted
- ☐ Lower development costs
- ☐ Lower operating costs
- ☐ Satisfaction of personnel
- ☐ Other (Please specify)

76. What were the disadvantages of agile methods compared to traditional methods?

☐ Documentation of poorer quality

☐ Code of lower quality

☐ Architecture more poorly structured

☐ Creation of technical debt

☐ More refactoring

☐ Difficulty in committing to project parameters

☐ Higher development costs

☐ Higher operating costs

☐ Other (Please specify)

77. Are all the software projects in this organization done using agile methods?

◯ Yes

◯ No

Implementing Agile Methods in a Traditional Context

78. Are there clear rules for deciding which projects will be done using agile methods?

◯ Yes

◯ No

79. What are the characteristics of projects done using agile methods?

- [ ] Small projects
- [ ] Simple projects
- [ ] New systems
- [ ] Stable architecture
- [ ] High rate of change
- [ ] Simple governance rules
- [ ] Independent of other systems in the organization
- [ ] Decomposable projects
- [ ] Projects that involve only one organizational unit
- [ ] Human resources that are geographically close
- [ ] Human resources available full-time
- [ ] Capacity of people to work on teams
- [ ] Technical competency
- [ ] Capacity of people to fill multiple roles
- [ ] Low risk
- [ ] Client acceptance of agile methods
- [ ] Wish of personnel to use agile methods
- [ ] Other characteristics (Please specify)

80. Did the implementation of agile methods start with pilot projects?

- ○ Yes
- ○ No

81. How was the implementation of agile on large projects managed?

Top-down			As much top-down as bottom-up			Bottom-up
1	2	3	4	5	6	7
O	O	O	O	O	O	O

82. What was the level of management support for the implementation?

	Very weak			Average			Very strong
	1	2	3	4	5	6	7
By upper management	O	O	O	O	O	O	O
By the management of IT	O	O	O	O	O	O	O
By business unit managers	O	O	O	O	O	O	O
Project personnel	O	O	O	O	O	O	O

83. Was the implementation accompanied by resources for organizational change management? These resources may include training, coaches, and change agents.

No resources			Moderate level of resources			Very significant resources
1	2	3	4	5	6	7
O	O	O	O	O	O	O

84. What organizational characteristics supported the implementation of agile methods?

☐ An organizational culture that values delegation

☐ An organizational culture that values autonomy

☐ An organizational culture that values flexibility

☐ An organizational culture that includes the right to make mistakes

☐ An organizational culture that values transparency

☐ An organizational culture that values objective measures of performance

☐ Poor performance of traditional projects

☐ A good understanding of agile methods by all participants

☐ Management support

☐ Acceptance by the client

☐ Acceptance by the IT department

☐ Personnel who wish to work using agile methods

☐ Availability of human and financial resources to support the implementation

☐ Other characteristics (Please specify)

85. What organizational characteristics are obstacles to the implementation of agile methods?

☐ A command and control management style

☐ An organizational culture that values standardized processes

☐ An organizational culture that values detailed processes

☐ Project approval processes that require the project parameters be well defined in advance

☐ Lack of adhesion of middle managers

☐ Lack of adhesion of project managers

☐ Lack of understanding of agile methods

☐ The desire of personnel to work with traditional methods

☐ Role definitions that are not aligned with agile methods

☐ Other (Please specify)

86. What performance objectives motivated the decision to use agile methods?

- [ ] More rapid delivery to customers
- [ ] Better adapted to customer needs
- [ ] Development of fewer features that are never used
- [ ] More centered on the creation of business value
- [ ] Better prioritization
- [ ] Code of better quality
- [ ] Documentation that is better adapted
- [ ] Lower development costs
- [ ] Lower operating costs
- [ ] Other (Please specify)

[   ]

87. What organizational change objectives motivated the decision to use agile methods?

☐ Better collaboration among organizational units

☐ Better communication and understanding between developers and end users

☐ Improved collaboration between development teams

☐ Change in leadership style from command and control to servant leadership

☐ Increased motivation and commitment of personnel

☐ Empowerment of personnel

☐ Better organizational climate

☐ Improved software engineering practices

☐ Other (Please specify)

88. Which of these organizational changes actually took place?

☐ Better collaboration among organizational units

☐ Better communication and understanding between developers and end users

☐ Improved collaboration between development teams

☐ Change in leadership style from command and control to servant leadership

☐ Increased motivation and commitment of personnel

☐ Empowerment of personnel

☐ Better organizational climate

☐ Improved software engineering practices

☐ Other (Please specify)

```



```

89. Which organizational roles were modified by the implementation of agile methods?

☐ Committees that approve projects

☐ Steering committees

☐ Managers

☐ Sponsors

☐ Project managers

☐ Architects

☐ Business analysts

☐ Functional analysts

☐ Developers

☐ Testers

☐ Quality assurance officers

☐ Integrators

☐ Documentarists

☐ Other (Please specify)

```

```

90. How did the transition from traditional to agile methods affect the role of the project manager?

- ☐ No effect on the project manager role.
- ☐ The project manager role has been abolished.
- ☐ The project manager does less detailed planning; it was done by the development teams.
- ☐ The project manager does less to coordinate teams.
- ☐ The project manager does more to coordinate teams.
- ☐ The project manager role is more strategic.
- ☐ The project managers do more stakeholder management.
- ☐ Other (Please specify)

> [   ]

91. For those who are new to the PO role, what are their biggest challenges?

- ☐ Understanding the new role
- ☐ Lack of decision-making authority
- ☐ Delays in responses to questions
- ☐ Pressure to produce the user stories of the next sprint
- ☐ Other (Please specify)

About the Authors

DR. BRIAN HOBBS, PMP, founded the Project Management Chair at the University of Quebec at Montreal in 2007, which he held until 2015. He holds a bachelor's degree in Industrial Engineering and an MBA and PhD in Management. He has been a professor at the School of Management of the University of Quebec at Montreal in the master's program in Project Management for more than 30 years. This program, of which he is a past director, is accredited by PMI's Global Accreditation Center. He has served terms on both PMI's Standards and Research Members Advisory Groups and is currently a member of the PMI-Montreal Board of Governors. He received the 2012 PMI Research Achievement Award. In 2012, he received the International Project Management Association Research Award with his colleague Monique Aubry for their work on project management offices (PMOs). In 2013, he received the Research Career Achievement Award from the School of Management. In 2015, he became a PMI Fellow.

YVAN PETIT, MENG, MBA (INSEAD), PhD, PMP, PfMP, has been an associate professor at the École des Sciences de la Gestion—University of Quebec at Montreal (ESG UQAM) since 2010. His research interests are in portfolio management, agile, and uncertainty management. He has more than 25 years of experience in project management, primarily in software development and R&D in the telecommunications industry. He has been a member of the Canadian committee on ISO/TC 258 Project, program, and portfolio management and is now a member of the PMI Standards Member Advisory Group. He is the program director for the postgraduate programs in project management at ESG UQAM.